I0152355

Guide

to

Vintage

Coin Folders

and

Albums

Thomas Moll

© 2007 by Thomas Moll
All rights reserved. No part of this book may be
reproduced in any form or by any electronic or
mechanical means, including information storage and
retrieval systems, without permission in writing from the
author.

Library of Congress Card Catalog Number:
ISBN: 978-0-6151-8887-4

Printed in the United States of America

To my two little numismatists

Contents

Illustrations

Acknowledgements

This work represents my passion for numismatics, and would not have come to fruition without the aid of others. Two fellow numismatists helped me acquire examples of vintage coin folders. Donald Ion of Rotorua, New Zealand found several Bertrand and Warrior folders for me. Viki Marleheim of Malmö, Sweden was instrumental in helping me acquire many Scandia folders. In addition, I owe a debt of gratitude to my friends Micah and Joy Rampulla for their expertise in preparing the photographs for the cover of the book. Finally, I must thank my wife for her constant patience and support of my various writing projects.

Introduction

A t the age of eight, I received my first group of
Whitman coin folders: five used albums that my
grandmother had picked up at a white elephant sale for $1.
Although I had been collecting coins for nearly a year, I had
kept my growing collection in an old cigar box. The five
folders that my grandmother purchased – for Lincoln cents,
Washington quarters, and Liberty Walking halves – housed
my coins. As I grew and added coins to my collection, I
acquired more coin folders. As a young adult I discovered the
coin folders produced for British coins, and set out to acquire
them to contain my British coin collection. Since that time I
have continued to seek out and obtain such folders to hold my
various coin collections and for the sheer joy of learning more
about them.

The Folders and Albums

The coin folders and albums discussed in this guide
were produced in what I consider the heyday of coin
collecting: the years following World War II up to the mid-
1980s. By tracing the number and types of coin albums
produced, it appears that the demand for albums grew during
the 1950s, peaked in the 1960s, and began a slow decline into
the 1980s. Many of the folders and albums mentioned in this
work have been out of print for nearly forty years.

There were two types of early coin housing systems. I
have decided to call them *folders* and *albums*. Coin folders
were the less expensive alternative, and consisted of cardboard
pages that had openings, or ports, punched in them to hold the

coins. The ports were the exact size of the coin and coins were retained in the holes by friction. The pages were glued to a backer sheet that was made of heavy paper. Thus, only one side of the coin was visible. For that reason, many folders had ports labeled for the placement of extra coins to exhibit the side hidden by the backer sheet. The pages could be folded one over the other to form a compact folder. When open completely, the folder lay flat and all coins were visible at once.

The coin albums were of sturdier construction. The pages contained ports to hold the coins, which were held in place by acetate sleeves on either side. Both sides of the coin could be viewed by turning the page. Several pages were bound into a binder made of heavy board and covered with a leatherette material. In early albums the pages were bound into the cover with staples; later albums used posts and screws.

The two largest manufacturers of coin folders and albums in the United States were Whitman and Dansco. Whitman Publishing Company of Racine, Wisconsin published both coin folders and albums. The coin folders measured 5¾ by 7½ inches when closed. All consisted of three blue cardboard pages glued to a darker blue cover. The cover was lettered in silver; internal labels were printed in black. Every Whitman folder included a leaf of paper that contained information about the coins contained therein.

Whitman albums were larger than the folders, measuring 7 by 8 ⁷⁄₈ inches. They had two, three, or four pages which were bound into the cover. The pages were cardboard covered with blue leatherette paper. Acetate slides protected both sides of the coins. Openings were labeled in gold, as was the cover. The cover was made of blue leatherette paper, and the spine was labeled in gold.

The Daniel Stamp Company of Venice, California, commonly called Dansco, also produced folders and albums to house coin collections. The Dansco folders measured 6½ by 9¼ inches when closed. Like the Whitman folders, pages were cardboard and contained ports to hold the coins. The pages were light gray and were labeled in black ink. The covers consisted of a brown leatherette material labeled in gold. Unlike Whitman folders, the Dansco folders were produced with two, three, four, or five pages.

During the 1950s Dansco produced a series of albums under the heading *Continental Line*. These Continental Line albums are extremely difficult to find, and I have only seen two examples. These albums had red pages, and the coins were held in the ports by acetate sleeves. The binder was red and labeled in gold. Pages were held in the binder using posts and screws.

The Price Guide

A majority of the folders and albums listed below have been out of print for thirty to forty years. They can still be found at a few coin dealers who have kept old stock, and they can also be found on popular internet auction sites.

The price guide for each folder or album is given as a range, such as $3 - $5 for a folder. The lower price is what someone could expect to pay for a folder in good, useable condition. The higher price is what one might expect to pay for a like-new example. The price range was taken from averaging actual dealer advertisements and prices realized at auctions. Since these items are no longer produced, it is a seller's market. I have seen some vintage albums top $40 at auction, and some folders exceed $20. An item identified as *not seen* means that I have never seen that particular folder or album available for sale. Information about these items was obtained from original sales literature and in most cases, from direct observation of the folders and albums themselves.

Part I

The Guide:
Descriptions and Prices

The following guide contains descriptions of countries for which specific coin folders or albums were produced. For each country there is a brief introduction to its coinage and a description of the items produced to house those coins. A price range is given for each folder or album.

It is important to remember that most of these folders and albums have been out of print for nearly forty years! The price given is what one may expect to pay for such an album or folder on the secondary market, i.e., internet auctions or second-hand dealers. The lower price represents what one might pay for a good, useable example; a new or lightly-used example might bring the upper price.

Although some of these products are difficult to find, there are some coin dealers who have original folders lurking in their shops, often at reasonable prices. I have seen a set of Whitman folders for Liberty Seated Quarters, numbers 9033 and 9034, sell for nearly $20 on a popular internet auction site. The same two folders were listed by a coin dealer on his website for $2.99 each. As with any out-of-print item, it pays to look around before you buy.

Australia

Australia issued its first series of coins in 1910. Threepences, sixpences, shillings, and florins were first struck in 1910; pennies and halfpennies followed in 1911. A five shilling piece was issued in 1937 and 1938. Coins were struck in these denominations until the mid-1960s; decimal currency was issued beginning in 1966.

Folders and albums for the shillings and pence coinage were printed by four companies: Dansco, Hawthorn, Hendo, and Whitman.

Dansco Folders

Dansco produced a series of folders for the predecimal Australian coins. The folders measured 6½ by 9¼ inches, and were covered with a brown leatherette material. The Dansco logo was stamped in gold on the cover, followed by Australia and the denomination. The spine was labeled as well. The interior pages were gray; the ports were dated and mintage figures were given for each coin.

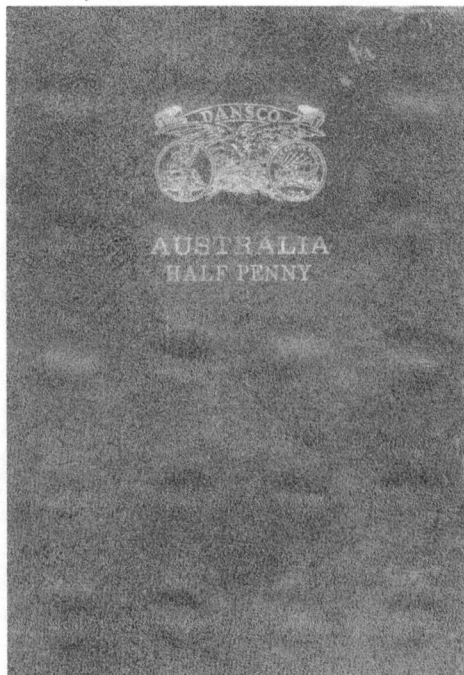

A Dansco halfpenny folder.

AUSTRALIA –

Dansco folders:		*Price guide:*
330	Halfpenny	$5 - $7
331	Penny	$5 - $7
332	Threepence and Sixpence	$5 - $7
333	Shilling	$5 - $7
334	Florin	$5 - $7
337	Australia type coins	$10 - $12
	General penny	$10 - $12

*The above album was blank.
The example that I have seen
did not have a stock number.*

Dansco produced similar folders for the decimal coinage:

Dansco folders:	*Price guide:*
One cent and two cents	$4 - $6
Five cents and ten cents	$4 - $6
Twenty cents and fifty cents	$4 - $6

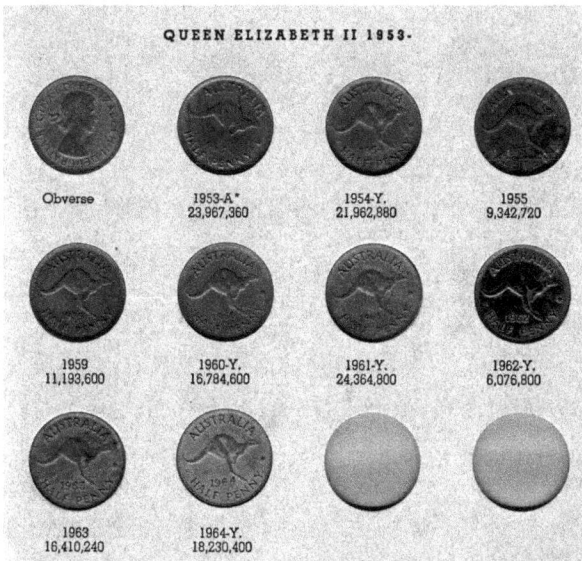

Halfpennies housed in a Dansco folder for Australian coins.

3

AUSTRALIA –

Hawthorn Press Folders

A series of folders entitled *The Australian Coin Album* was produced by the Hawthorn Press of Melbourne. The company was a premier publisher in Australia before being destroyed by fire in 1971. The folders measured 6½ by 9¼ inches when closed. The openings were dated and included the mintage of each coin.

Empty folders produced by Hawthorn have been listed on internet auction sites based in Australia and they have fetched between ten and fifteen Australian dollars each.

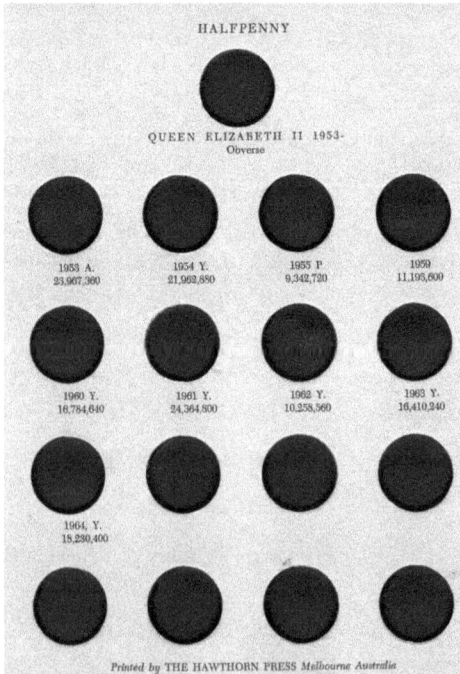

The fourth page of the Hawthorn Press halfpenny folder, designed to hold the coins issued during the reign of Elizabeth II.

Hawthorn Press Folders:	*Price Guide:*
Halfpenny	$8 - $10
Penny	$8 - $10
Threepence and Sixpence	$8 - $10
Shilling	not seen
Florin	not seen

4

AUSTRALIA –

Hendo Folders

Coin folders printed under the title *Australian Coin Album* were produced by Hendo. The folders measured 6½ by 9⅛ inches and contained three pages. The pages were made of gray cardboard. The ports were labeled in black ink with the date and mintage. The folders were covered in a heavy faux leatherette material. The covers were stamped in gold with the Hendo logo, *Australian Coin Album*, and the denomination.

Empty Hendo folders have been listed in Australian auction catalogs and on internet auction sites based in Australia. They have fetched between ten and fifteen Australian dollars each.

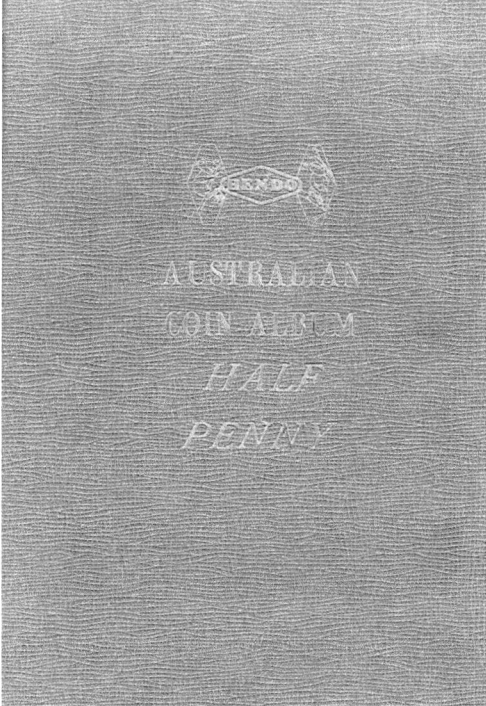

Cover of a Hendo halfpenny album. The Hendo logo at the top includes a koala and a kookaburra.

Hendo folders:	Price guide:
Halfpenny	$6 - $8
Penny	not seen
Threepence and Sixpence	$6 - $8
Shilling	not seen
Florin	$10 - $12

AUSTRALIA –

Whitman Folders and Albums

A series of eleven folders was published by Whitman for Australian coins. The folders were produced in the usual format: blue cover, silver lettering on the cover, and a description of the coins on the overleaf. The coin folders measured 5¾ by 7½ inches when closed. There were spaces for obverse coins. Whitman produced two albums for Australian type collections as well.

Whitman folders:		*Price guide:*
9661	Halfpennies 1911-1936	$5 - $10
9662	Halfpennies 1938-1964	$5 - $10
9663	Pennies 1911-1936	$5 - $10
9664	Pennies 1938-1952	$5 - $10
9665	Pennies 1953-1964	$5 - $10
9666	Threepence 1910-1964	$5 - $10
9667	Sixpence 1910-1963	$5 - $10
9668	Shillings 1910-1936	$5 - $10
9669	Shillings 1938-1963	$5 - $10
9670	Florins 1910-1936	$5 - $10
9671	Florins and Crowns 1937-1963	$5 - $10

Whitman albums:		*Price guide:*
9527	Type, bronze and decimal coins	not seen
9528	Type, silver coins	not seen

AUSTRALIA –

AUSTRALIAN FLORINS AND CROWNS
GEORGE VI—1936-1952

| 1938 | 1939 | 1940 |
| 2,990,000 | 630,000 | 8,410,000 |

| 1941 | 1942 |
| 7,614,000 | 18,154,000 |

| 1942-S | 1943 |
| 6,000,000 | 12,562,000 |

| 1943-S | 1944 | 1944-S |
| 11,000,000 | 22,440,000 | 11,000,000 |

No. 9671

The first page of Whitman folder 9671 – Australian florins and crowns.

British Commonwealth

Whitman Publishing Company produced three folders entitled *British Commonwealth*, for farthing-, halfpenny-, and penny-sized coins. Given the large number of British colonies and the variety of colonial coinages, Whitman recognized the utility of creating such a series of folders. All folders in this series were blank, allowing the collector to label them as he wished.

Whitman Folders:		Price guide:
9672	Farthing size - 48 ports	$3 - $10
9673	Halfpenny size - 36 ports	$3 - $10
9674	Penny size – 36 ports	$5 - $15

See also GREAT BRITAIN.

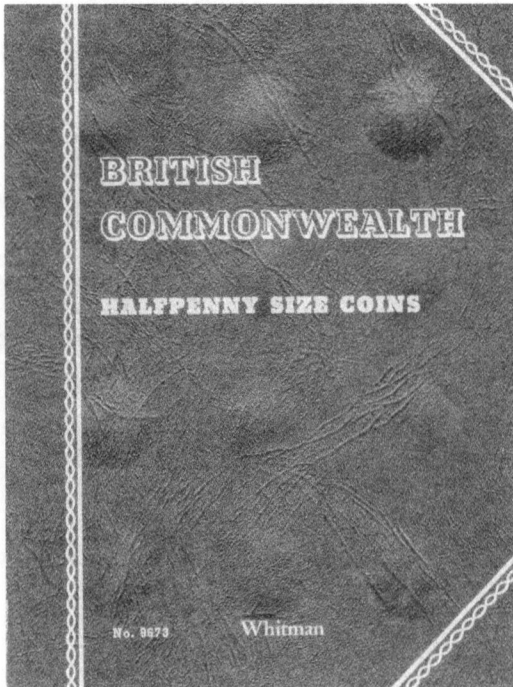

Cover of Whitman folder 9673, which was designed to hold halfpenny size coins of British Commonwealth countries.

British North America

During the 1860s, the Maritime Colonies of British North America began to issue coins. Coins were struck for Nova Scotia and New Brunswick beginning in 1861, followed by Newfoundland in 1865. Prince Edward Island issued a one cent piece in 1871. Nova Scotia and New Brunswick were part of the Canadian Confederation in 1867, and Prince Edward Island joined in 1873. Therefore, the coinages of those colonies were short-lived. Newfoundland, however, remained a separate colony and continued to issue its own coins.

Whitman published a folder entitled *Cents and Half Cents of British North America*, which was part of the Newfoundland series of coin folders. The first folder listed below contained ports for the half cent and cent coins issued by New Brunswick, Nova Scotia, and Prince Edward Island. The higher denomination coins issued by New Brunswick could be housed in the second folder. This folder bore the title *Newfoundland Five Cents* even though an entire page was devoted to the coins issued by New Brunswick.

Whitman folder:		Price guide:
9074	Cents and half cents of British North America	$3 - $5
9075	Newfoundland five cents, 1865-1947	$3 - $5
	The above folder includes ports for the five, ten, and twenty cent coins issued by New Brunswick in 1862 and 1864.	

See also NEWFOUNDLAND.

9

BRITISH NORTH AMERICA –

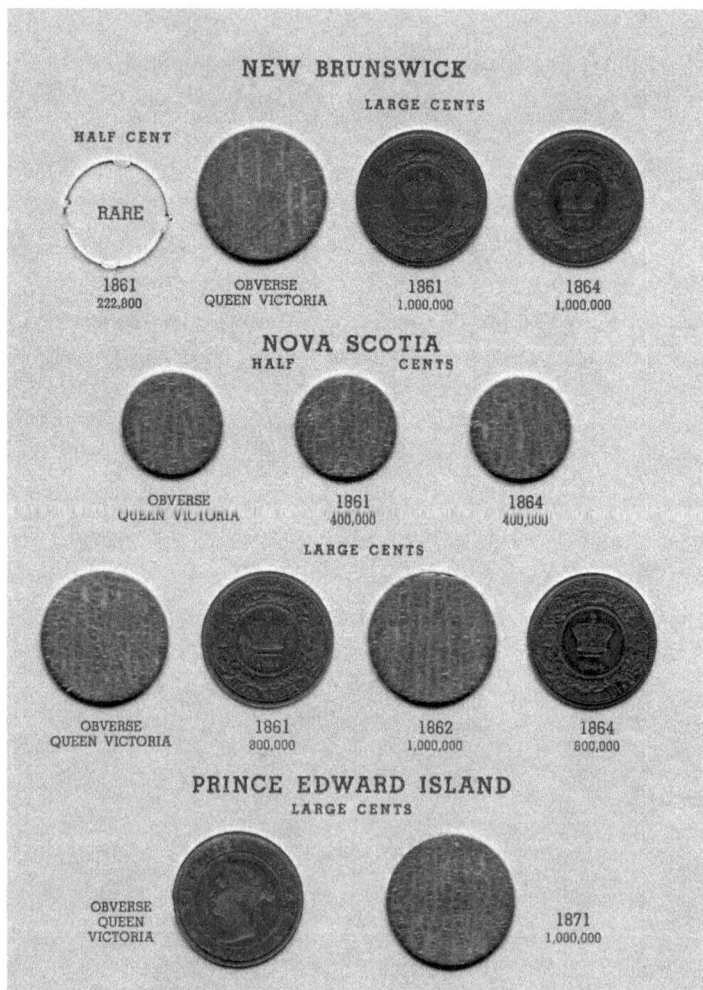

A page from Whitman folder 9074 – Cents and half cents of British North America. This page could house the coins issued by New Brunswick, Nova Scotia, and Prince Edward Island.

Canada

The Province of Canada, present-day Ontario and Québec, issued decimal coins beginning in 1858. At that time four denominations were struck: one cent, five cent, ten cent, and twenty cent coins. At about the same time the other British colonies in North America – Nova Scotia, New Brunswick, and Prince Edward Island – issued their own coins. The above-mentioned colonies united to form the Dominion of Canada in 1867. In 1870, the new nation issued coins that resembled the earlier issues of 1858. In 1870, however, five coins were issued: one cent, five cents, ten cents, twenty-five cents, and fifty cents. A dollar coin did not appear until 1935.

Folders for the coins of Canada were produced by both Dansco and Whitman; Whitman also produced albums.

Dansco Folders

A series of folders for Canadian coins was manufactured by Dansco. The folders were covered with brown leatherette material and labeled in gold on the cover. The interior pages were gray; the ports were dated and mintage figures were given. Dansco folders measured 6½ by 9¼ inches.

Dansco folders:		*Price guide:*
200	Small cents 1858-	$3 - $5
201	Five cents 1858-	$3 - $5
202	Ten cents 1858-	$3 - $5
203	Twenty-five cents 1858-1952	$4 - $8
	The above folder includes two ports for the twenty cent piece of 1858.	
204	Fifty cents 1870-1952	$4 - $8
	Dollars 1935-	$4 - $8
210	Canada type set to circa 1965	$5 - $10

CANADA –

Whitman Folders and Albums

A series of twenty folders was published by Whitman for Australian coins. The coin folders measured 5¾ by 7½ inches when closed, and were of the familiar blue variety. There were spaces for obverse coins. Whitman produced seventeen albums for Canadian coins, including an album to hold sealed mint sets.

Whitman folders:		*Price guide:*
9061	Large cents 1858-1920	$3 - $5
9062	Small cents 1920-	$3 - $5
9063	Silver five cents 1858-1921	$4 - $6
9064	Nickel five cents 1922-1960	$3 - $5
9089	Nickel five cents 1961-	$3 - $5
9065	Ten cents 1858-1936	$4 - $6
9066	Ten cents 1937-	$3 - $5
9067	Twenty-five cents 1858-1910	$4 - $6
	The above folder includes two ports for the twenty cent piece of 1858.	
9068	Twenty-five cents 1911-1952	$3 - $5
9069	Twenty-five cents 1953-	$3 - $5
9079	Twenty-five cents blank	$4 - $6
9070	Fifty cents 1870-1910	$4 - $6
9071	Fifty cents 1911-1936	$4 - $6
9072	Fifty cents 1937-1960	$3 - $5
9094	Fifty cents 1961-	$3 - $5
9080	Fifty cents blank	$4 - $6
9073	Dollars 1935-1957	$3 - $5
9087	Dollars 1958-	$3 - $5
9086	Dollars blank	$4 - $6
9081	Canada type coin collection	$4 - $6

CANADA –

CANADIAN QUARTERS
ELIZABETH II—1953-

Obverse

1953
Large Date
BOTH KINDS 10,456,769

1953
Small Date

1954
2,318,891

1955
9,552,505

1956
11,269,353

1957
12,770,180

1958

No. 9069

Whitman folder 9069, which can house Canadian twenty-five cents beginning with 1953. This folder was produced in the late 1950s; the majority of the ports in this folder are blank. This particular folder had enough ports to accommodate coins dated through 1984.

CANADA –

Whitman albums:		Price guide:
9500	Large cents 1858-1920	$5 - $8
9501	Small cents 1920-	$5 - $8
9502	Five cent silver 1858-1921	not seen
9503	Five cent nickel 1922-	$5 - $8
9504	Ten cents 1858-	not seen
9505	Twenty and twenty-five cents 1870-1936	not seen
9506	Twenty-five cents 1937-	$5 - $8
9507	Twenty-five cents blank	$5 - $8
9508	Fifty cents 1870-1936	not seen
9509	Fifty cents 1937-	$5 - $8
9510	Fifty cents blank	not seen
9511	Dollars 1935-1965	$5 - $8
9512	Dollars blank	not seen
9513	Type set	not seen
9522	Type set small denominations	$12 - $20
9521	Type set large denominations	$12 - $20
9515	Mint sealed mint sets	not seen

See also BRITISH NORTH AMERICA and NEWFOUNDLAND.

Cuba

Prior to the revolution in Cuba in 1959, there was a strong connection between Cuba and the United States. This was due no only to the close proximity of the two countries, but to the role that the United States played in helping gain Cuban independence from Spain. Coins denominated in pesos and centavos were issued beginning in 1915.

In the early 1960s Dansco produced a folder for the coinage of Cuba. Perhaps the success of the Mexican series of coin folders encouraged the company to produce type set folders for other Latin American countries. The Cuba folder was mentioned in sales literature, but I have never seen an example.

Dansco Folder: *Price Guide:*
240   Cuba type coins, 1915 -   not seen

Czechoslovakia

Czechoslovakia was a state formed after the First World War from parts of the Austro-Hungarian Empire. The country began to issue coins in 1921. The coinage consisted of the main currency unit, the *koruna*, which was divided into one hundred *haleru*. The coinage was a continuation of the old Austro-Hungarian currency system of *crowns* and *heller*. The first Czechoslovak coinage consisted of haleru and one koruna coins. A five korun coin appeared in 1925, followed by ten and twenty korun coins in the 1930s.

Dansco manufactured an album for the coins Czechoslovakia as part of its *Continental Line* of albums. The three-page album contained red pages that could hold examples of the circulating coins and commemoratives issued between 1922 and the 1950s. Ports were included for coins of the Czechoslovak Republic, the Slovak Republic, the Protectorate of Bohemia and Moravia, and the post World War II coinage.

Continental Line album:
Type coins 1918-1950s

Price guide:
not seen

Denmark

The decimal system was introduced in Denmark in 1873, when Denmark entered into a monetary union with neighboring Sweden. At that time Denmark adopted the *krone*, or crown, as its principle monetary unit. The krone was divided into 100 *øre*.

The Danish numismatist Frovin Sieg authored price guides to Danish and Scandinavian coins, and also produced a series of coin folders to house Danish coins. Eighteen folders were produced, including one folder for the gold coins issued by the kingdom. The folders measured 6⅝ by 8¾ inches, and were covered in a red, faux leather fabric. The covers were lettered in gold. Each album included a page that contained black-and-white photographs of each type of coin housed in the album, along with a brief description. The company also produced a slipcase that could hold seven albums.

In the early 1980s, the folders retailed for the equivalent of four to five dollars a piece. A decade later, the price had risen to the equivalent of seven dollars. The folders are difficult to find, and are listed occasionally on Danish internet auction websites.

1) 1888 Chr. IX 25 års regeringsjubilæum 15. november. Der er udmøntet 101.253.

3) 1903 Chr. IX 40 års regeringsjubilæum 15. november. Der er udmøntet 103.392.

Pictured at left is part of the overleaf from the Sieg folder for Danish commemorative coins. There is a photograph of each type, plus information on the event commemorated and the number of coins minted.

DENMARK –

Sieg folder:	*Price guide:*
1 øre 1874-1972	$7 - $10
2 øre 1874-1972	$7 - $10
5 øre 1874-1941	$7 - $10
5 øre 1941-1988	$7 - $10
10 øre and 25 øre 1874-1923	$7 - $10
10 øre 1924-1988	$7 - $10
25 øre 1924-1983	$7 - $10
25 øre and 50 øre 1973-	$7 - $10
Half and 1 krone 1875-1977	$7 - $10
1 krone Margarethe II	$5 - $7

> *This folder has unlabeled ports. One could use this as a continuation album for the one krone coins beginning 1978, or for a collection of one krone coins of Queen Margarethe II, whose coinage commenced in 1973.*

2 kroner 1875-1959	$9 - $12
5 kroner 1960-1988	$7 - $10
5, 10, and 20 kroner 1989-	$5 - $7
10 kroner 1979-1988	$5 - $7
Commemorative coins	$15 - $20
Gold 10 and 20 kroner, 1873-1931	not seen
Type coins, Kings Christian IX, Frederick VIII, and Christian X	not seen
Type coins, Kings Christian X and Frederick IX	not seen

DENMARK –

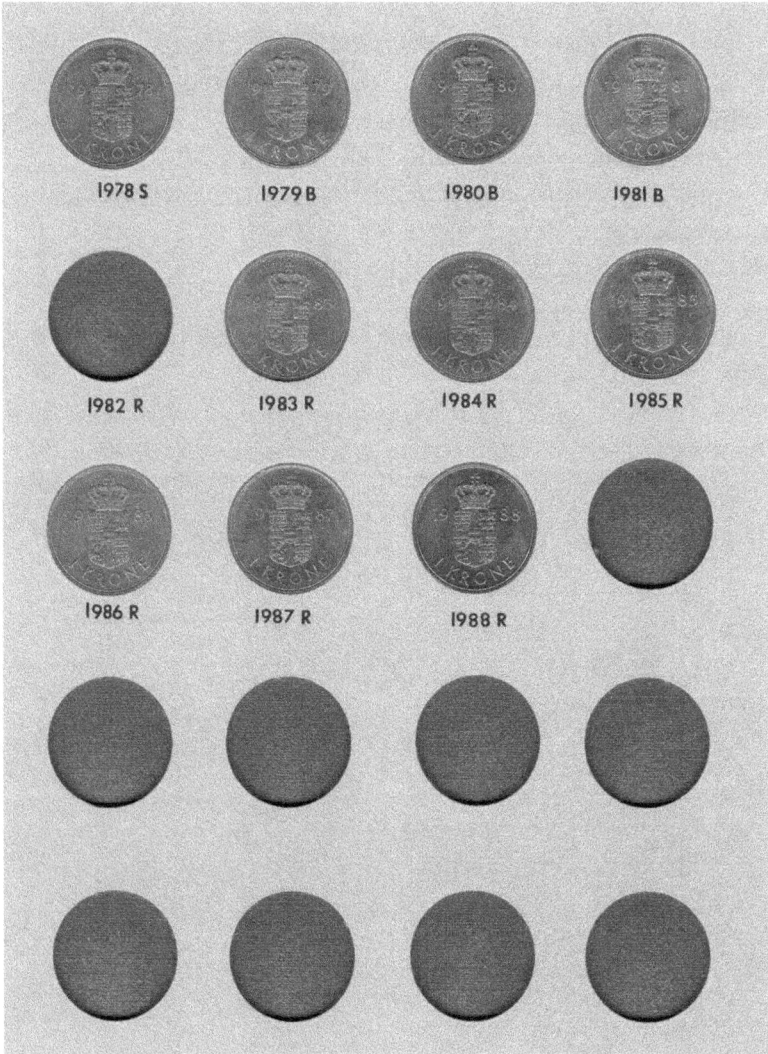

The unlabeled Sieg folder for the one krone coins of Queen Margarethe II. Dates were added by the author.

Fiji

Fiji, a group of islands in the Pacific Ocean, became a British crown colony in 1874. The colony used British coins until 1934, when Fiji issued a series of coins: halfpenny, penny, sixpence, shilling, and florin. A nickel-brass threepence was introduced in 1947. The last coins issued in the pence and shilling system were dated 1965. Coins in decimal currency were issued beginning in 1969.

Dansco manufactured a large, five-page folder that could house all of the pre-decimal coins issued by Fiji between 1934 and 1965.

Dansco folder: *Price guide:*
350   Fiji, complete collection $15 - $20

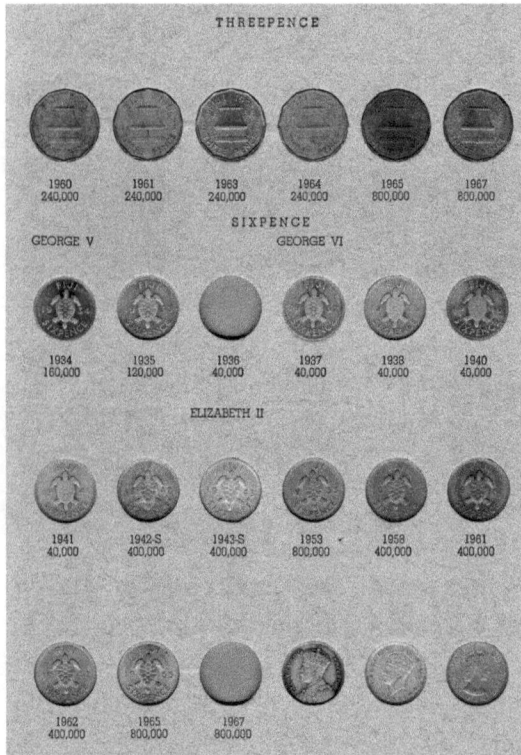

The third page of the Dansco coin folder for Fiji.

Great Britain

The United Kingdom of Great Britain and Ireland was the foremost colonial power in the world for several hundred years. The British Empire reached its zenith around 1900, when Queen Victoria reigned over one-quarter of the world's population. British merchants circled the globe, taking their pounds, shillings, and pence with them. The British retained their non-decimal currency system until they switched to a decimal system in 1971.

Whitman publishing produced a large series of folders and several albums to hold the imperial coinage of Great Britain. The "original series" of folders, as I call them, covered the six lowest denominations of coins, from farthing through shilling. These folders appeared in sales literature from the early 1960s, have stock numbers in the 9000 range, and were copyrighted by Whitman Publishing. The second series, which bore stock numbers in the 8000 range, were produced by Western Publishing (Whitman) in the late 1960s. Though manufactured in the United States, the folders were imprinted *Copyright [date] – Don Hirschhorn Limited – Newcastle upon Tyne.* This second series of folders included a large range of blank folders, which were extremely useful for collectors of British Colonial and Commonwealth coinage. Whitman also produced quite a few albums for British coins.

Given the fact that British coins were so ubiquitous during the Nineteenth and Twentieth Centuries, it is perplexing that Whitman was the only publisher to manufacture folders for British coinage.

GREAT BRITAIN –

Whitman folders:		Price guide:
9675	Farthings 1860-1901	$4 - $6
9676	Farthings 1902-1936	$3 - $5
9677	Farthings 1937-1956	$3 - $5
9672	Farthings, type	$3 - $5
8001	Farthings, blank – 48 openings	$4 - $6
9678	Halfpennies 1860-1901	$4 - $6
9679	Halfpennies 1902-1936	$3 - $5
9680	Halfpennies 1937-1967	$3 - $5
9673	Halfpennies, type	$3 - $5
8002	Halfpennies, blank – 36 openings	$4 - $6
9681	Pennies 1860-1880	$4 - $6
9682	Pennies 1881-1901	$4 - $6
9683	Pennies 1902-1929	$3 - $5
9684	Pennies 1930-1967	$3 - $5
8003	Pennies, blank – 36 openings	$4 - $6
9685	Threepence silver 1838-1901	$4 - $6
9686	Threepence silver 1902-1945	$4 - $6
9687	Threepence brass 1937-1967	$3 - $5
8004	Threepence brass, blank – 60 openings	$4 - $6
9689	Sixpence 1902-1936	$4 - $6
9690	Sixpence 1937-1967	$3 - $5
8005	Sixpence blank – 60 openings	$4 - $6
9693	Shillings 1902-1936	$4 - $6
9694	Shillings 1937-1951	$3 - $5
9695	Shillings 1953-1967	$3 - $5
8006	Shillings blank – 48 openings	$4 - $6
8009	Florins 1911-1940	$3 - $5
8010	Florins 1941-1967	$3 - $5
8011	Florins blank – 36 openings	$4 - $6
8012	Half crowns 1911-1940	$3 - $5
8013	Half crowns 1941-1967	$3 - $5
8008	Half crowns blank – 36 openings	$4 - $6

GREAT BRITAIN –

1923 6,382,793	**1924** 17,444,218	**1925** 12,720,558
1926 21,809,621	**1927** 8,939,873	**1928** 23,123,384
1929 28,319,326	**1930** 16,990,289	**1931** 16,873,268
1932 9,406,117	**1933** 22,185,083	**1934** 9,304,009
1935 13,995,621	Issued During Reign of EDWARD VIII	**1936** 24,380,171

Sixpences of King George V, housed in Whitman folder 9689.

GREAT BRITAIN –

Whitman albums:		Price guide:
9530	Farthings 1860-1901	not seen
9531	Farthings 1902-1956	$7 - $10
9532	Halfpennies 1860-1901	not seen
9533	Halfpennies 1902-1936	not seen
9534	Halfpennies 1937-	$7 - $10
9535	Pennies 1860-1901	not seen
9536	Pennies 1902-1936	not seen
9537	Pennies 1937-	$7 - $10
9520	Type – Queen Victoria 1837-1901	$12 - $20
9516	Type – minor coins 1902-	$12 - $20
9517	Type – silver coins 1902-	$12 - $20

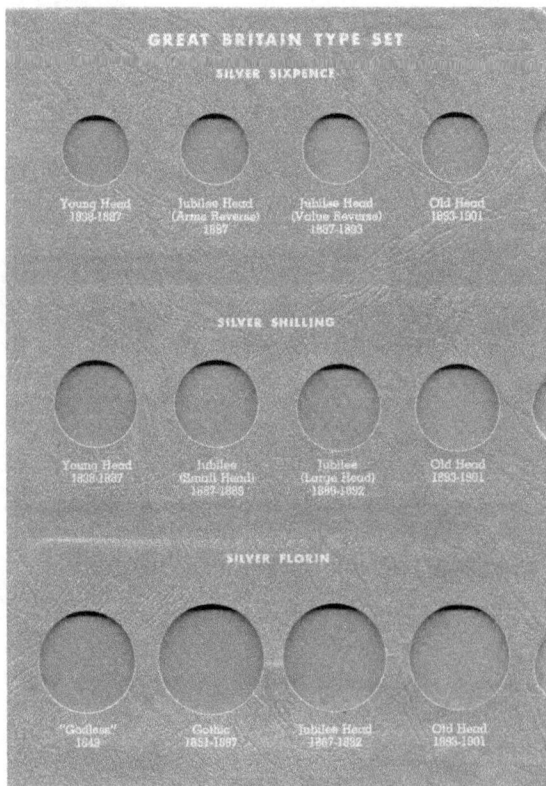

Whitman Album 9520, for type coins issued during the reign of Queen Victoria. The album had room for all the coins struck for circulation in Great Britain, plus Maundy sets and special denominations issued for colonial use.

Greenland

Frovin Sieg produced a folder to hold the coins issued by Greenland. It was listed in sales literature in the early 1980s priced at 30 kroner, but the folder disappeared from production shortly thereafter. There were eight different type coins issued in Greenland between 1926 and 1964, therefore this folder should have had at least eight ports.

Sieg folder:
Greenland coins

Price guide:
not seen

Guatemala

Guatemala declared its independence from Spain in 1821, and became an independent republic in 1839. At that time the country issued *pesos* which were divided into 8 *reales*. This monetary system continued intermittently until the early 1900s. New coins based on a decimal system were introduced in 1915. The decimal system continued after 1932, when the main currency unit was renamed the *Quetzal*.

In the early 1960s Dansco produced several folders for the coinage of various Latin American countries. The Guatemala folder was mentioned in sales literature, but I have never seen an example.

Dansco folder:

230   Guatemala type coins, 1915 -

Price guide:

not seen

Guernsey

Guernsey, one of the two bailiwicks that make up the Channel Islands, began to issue coins in the 1830s. The coins were denominated in *doubles*, where one double was the near equivalent to half of a farthing. Eight doubles, therefore, was the Guernsey equivalent of one penny.

According to other contemporary folders, Whitman Publishing (United Kingdom) produced three folders for the coins minted for Guernsey. By the descriptions of the folders, it would appear that ports for the 1966-dated coins (four doubles, eight doubles, threepence, and ten shillings) could not accommodated in these folders. The folders below have never been seen on the secondary market and should be considered extremely rare.

Whitman Folders:		*Price Guide*
8030	One & two doubles 1830-1929	not seen
8031	Four doubles 1864-1956	not seen
8032	Eight doubles, threepence 1864-1959	not seen

Hong Kong

Hong Kong, located off the southern coast of China, became a British possession in 1841. It was later created a crown colony, and a local decimal coinage was issued beginning in 1863. The British leased more territory from China in 1898 under a 99-year lease. When the lease expired in 1997, the whole colony was returned to China. Hong Kong continues to issue its own coins and banknotes, as it is a special region of China.

Dansco issued a three-page folder to hold a type collection of Hong Kong coins. The folder contained twenty-nine ports, and could hold examples of the coins issued during the reigns of Queen Victoria, King Edward VII, King George V, King George VI, and Queen Elizabeth II. The folder was produced in the mid-1960s and only had ports for the five cent, ten cent, fifty cent, and dollar coins issued in the 1960s. The newer issues of Queen Elizabeth II, including the twenty cent and two dollar coins, cannot be housed in this folder.

Dansco Folder: *Price Guide:*
450   Hong Kong type, 1863-1960s $8 - $10

28

HONG KONG –

QUEEN ELIZABETH 1952-

5 Cents 1958-
Nickel Brass

10 Cents 1955-
Nickel Brass

50 Cents 1958-
Copper Nickel

One Dollar 1960-
Copper Nickel

A type collection of Hong Kong coins issued early in the reign of Queen Elizabeth II. These are the only coins of Queen Elizabeth II that can be housed in Dansco folder 450, which was produced in the mid-1960s.

Iceland

Iceland has been linked with Denmark since 1380. It was established as an independent kingdom in personal union with the Danish Crown in 1918. The country issued its own coinage beginning in 1922. At that time, the main currency unit remained the crown: *krona* in Icelandic. The krona was divided into 100 aurar. Iceland became an independent republic in 1944.

Given the long political relationship between Denmark and Iceland, it is not surprising that Frovin Sieg produced folders to house a collection of Icelandic coinage. Four such folders listed in sales literature in the early 1980s priced at 35 Danish kroner each. The folders were identical to those produced by Sieg for Danish coins; they had red covers, were lettered in gold, and contained an informational page on the coins.

Sieg folder:	*Price Guide:*
King Christian X, coins issued 1922-1942	not seen
Republic, coins of 1, 5, 10, 25, 50 aurar and 2 krónur, 1946-1980	$10 - $12
Republic, coins of 1, 5, 10, and 50 krónur, 1946-1980	$10 - $12
Republic – Commemorative coins	not seen

ICELAND –

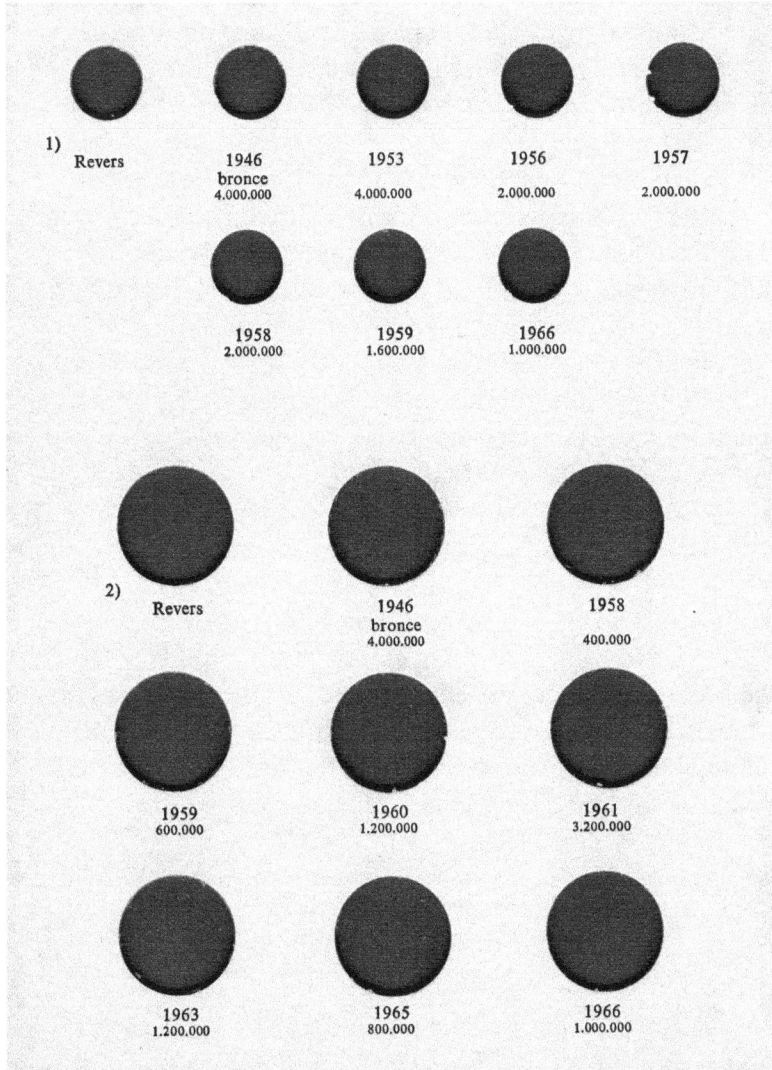

1) Revers	1946 bronce 4.000.000	1953 4.000.000	1956 2.000.000	1957 2.000.000
	1958 2.000.000	1959 1.600.000	1966 1.000.000	

2) Revers	1946 bronce 4.000.000	1958 400.000
1959 600.000	1960 1.200.000	1961 3.200.000
1963 1.200.000	1965 800.000	1966 1.000.000

First page of the Sieg folder for Icelandic coins of one and five aurar.

Ireland

Ireland, which forms part of the British Isles, was part of the United Kingdom from 1801 until 1922. At that time, a majority of the Irish counties formed the independent Irish Free State.

The Irish Free State issued the first modern Irish coinage beginning in 1928. An Irish harp graced the obverse of all the coins. The coinage was based on the pounds-shillings-pence system used in Great Britain, and most of the new Irish coins were identical in size to their British equivalents. Only the Irish threepence and sixpence coins differed; they were slightly larger than their British counterparts. This series of coins ended in 1969, as Ireland prepared to switch to decimal coinage.

Three companies – Dansco, ICC, and Whitman – produced folders to accommodate Irish coins.

Dansco Folders

Three folders for Irish coinage were produced by Dansco. The folders were mentioned in sales literature, but an actual set has never been seen. The folders were probably identical to other Dansco folders of the era: brown leatherette cover, measuring 6½ by 9¼ inches when closed.

Dansco folders:		*Price guide:*
371	Farthings, halfpennies, and pennies	not seen
372	Threepence, sixpence, and shillings	not seen
373	Florins and half crowns	not seen

32

IRELAND –

Irish Coin Library

A three-volume set of folders for Irish coins was produced by International Coins and Currency. The folders measured 6½ by 9¼ and were covered in a light green leatherette material. The outside of each folder was stamped *Irish Coin Library* in gold, which included an Irish harp motif. The spine of each volume was labeled *Irish Coin Library* with the volume number. The Irish Coin Library albums appeared to be close to their Dansco counterparts; perhaps Dansco published them as a specialty item for International Coins and Currency.

Irish Coin Library folder:		*Price guide:*
I	Farthings, halfpennies, and pennies	$15 - $20
II	Threepence, sixpence, and shillings	$15 - $20
III	Florins and half crowns	$15 - $20

Volume III has a port for the ten shilling commemorative coin issued in 1966.

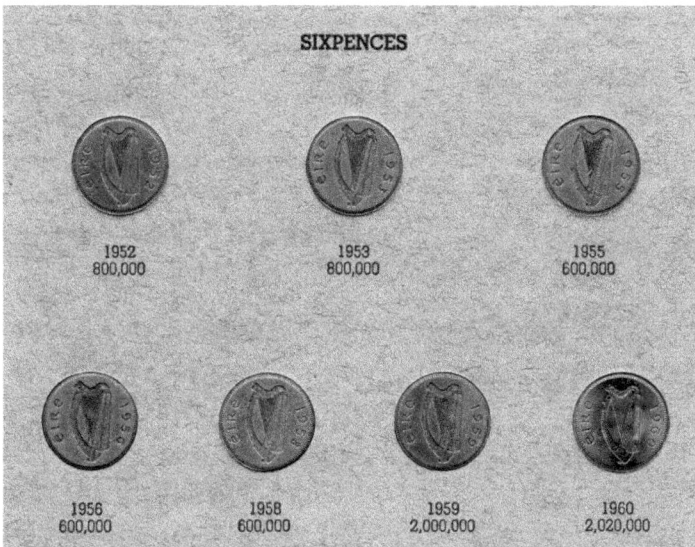

A page of Irish sixpences from volume II of the Irish Coin Library.

33

IRELAND –

Whitman Folders

The Whitman Publishing Company (United Kingdom) produced a series of folders to hold Irish coins. The folders are similar in size and format to other Whitman coin folders, but were made with distinctive green covers. The outside lettering was in silver shadow letters. The farthing folder was produced with only two pages, unlike any other Whitman folder. The set of folders observed was produced in 1970. These folders are difficult to find in any condition.

Folders:		*Price Guide*
8020	Farthings 1928-1959	$15 - $20
8021	Halfpennies 1929-1967	$15 - $20
8022	Pennies 1928-1968	not seen
8023	Threepence 1928-1968	$15 - $20
8024	Sixpence 1928-1968	$15 - $20

The last Irish sixpence was dated 1969. There is no port in this folder to accommodate that date per se, but the 1969 sixpence could be placed in the obverse port.

8025	Shillings, 1928-1968	$15 - $20
8026	Florins, 1928-1968	not seen
8027	Half Crowns, 1928-1967	$15 - $20

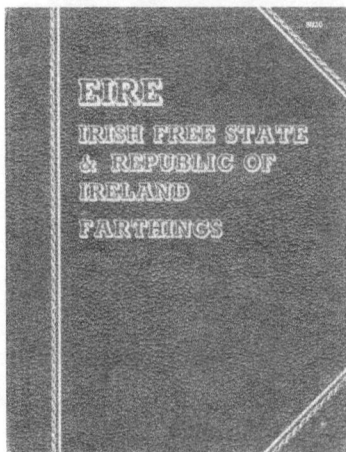

Whitman folder 8020, for Irish farthings. This was a two-page folder, and unlike other Whitman folders, was covered in green leatherette paper.

Israel

The State of Israel gained its independence in 1948, and the new nation began issuing coins. The Israeli pound was divided into 1,000 *prutot*. A currency reform was instituted in 1960, where the *lira* (pound) was divided into 100 *agorot*.

A folder for type coins of the State of Israel was produced by Dansco in the 1960s.

Dansco folder: *Price Guide:*
600   Israel type coins, 1948-   not seen

Japan

Japan modernized its currency system after the Shogunate was abolished in 1867. The old system, in which the value of a coin was based on weight and fineness, was abandoned for a "modern" currency system based on Occidental ideas concerning currency systems and other financial principles. The *yen* was introduced in 1870 and subdivided into 100 *sen*; a sen was in turn divided into 10 *rin*.

A folder was produced by Dansco to hold a type collection of Japanese coins beginning in 1870. The folder was produced in the early 1960s, and can accommodate type coins issued up to that period.

Dansco folder: *Price guide:*
460   Japan type coins, 1870- $20 - $30

Jersey

Jersey, part of the Channel Islands, struck minor coins to British standards since the mid-nineteenth century. Those coins were denominated in fractions of a shilling.

According to other contemporary folders, Whitman Publishing (United Kingdom) produced two folders for bronze coins minted for Jersey. Ports for the quarter shilling (1957-1966) and five shilling coin (1966) do not appear to be included in either folder. The folders have never been seen on the secondary market; they are exceedingly rare.

Whitman folders:		*Price guide:*
8028	$^1/_{26}$th & $^1/_{24}$th shilling, 1866-1947	not seen
8029	$^1/_{13}$th & $^1/_{12}$th shilling, 1877-1966	not seen

Mexico

With the advent of the United Mexican States in 1905, a new system of coinage was introduced. The nation continued to use the *peso*, which was divided into 100 *centavos*. A new series of coins was introduced at that time.

Coin folders were produced for Mexican coins by both Dansco and Whitman.

COINS OF MEXICO
ONE CENTAVO
1899—First year of Mexico Small Centavo. Reads Republica Mexicana on Reverse. Issued by two different mints.   M—Mexico City   C—Culiacan

Rare			
1899-M 51,000	1900-M 4,010,000	1901-M 1,494,000	1901-C 220,000
1902-M 2,090,000	1902-C 320,000	1903-M 8,400,000	1903-C 536,200
1904-M 10,250,000	1904-C 147,500	1905-M 3,643,000	1905-C 110,000

1905—FIRST YEAR OF 1c OF THE ESTADOS UNIDOS MEXICANOS
TYPE I

Obverse	1905 6,040,000	1906 67,505,000	1910 8,700,000
1911 16,450,000	1912 12,850,000	1913 12,650,000	1914 17,350,000

ISSUED BY REVOLUTIONARY FORCES OF ZAPATA
AT THE MEXICO CITY MINT
TYPE II

1915 178,048

The Dansco folder for one centavo coins of Mexico.

MEXICO –

Dansco produced a wider range of folders. The one centavo folder contained ports for coins dated 1899 and after; in the other folders the ports begin with the coinage of 1905. Whitman produced three folders to hold one and five centavo coins, and an album for Mexican type coins.

Dansco folders:		Price guide:
227	One centavo 1899 –	$5 - $7
221	Five centavo 1905 – 1969	$5 - $7
222	Ten centavo	not seen
223	Twenty centavo	not seen
225	Fifty centavo	not seen
224	One peso	not seen
226	Two, five, ten pesos	not seen
220	Type set 1905-	not seen

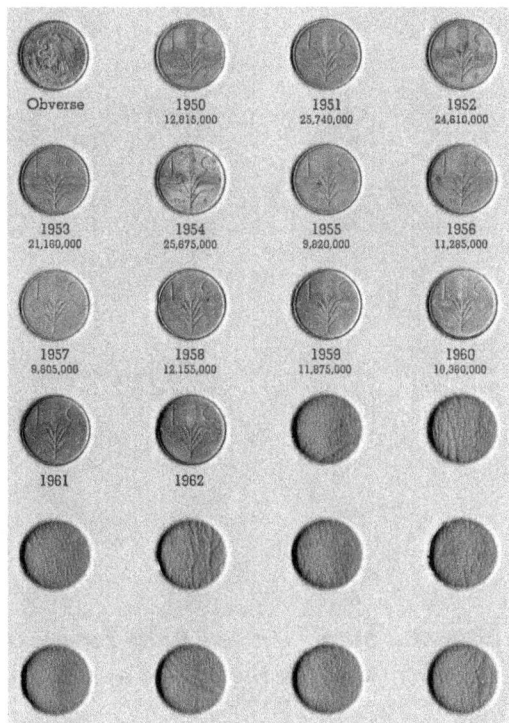

Mexican one centavo coins housed in Whitman folder 9696.

MEXICO –

Whitman folders:		Price guide:
9696	One centavo 1905 -	$4
9697	Five centavos 1905-1955	$4
9698	Five centavos 1954-	$4

Whitman album:		Price guide:
9524	Mexican type set 1905-	$12 - $20

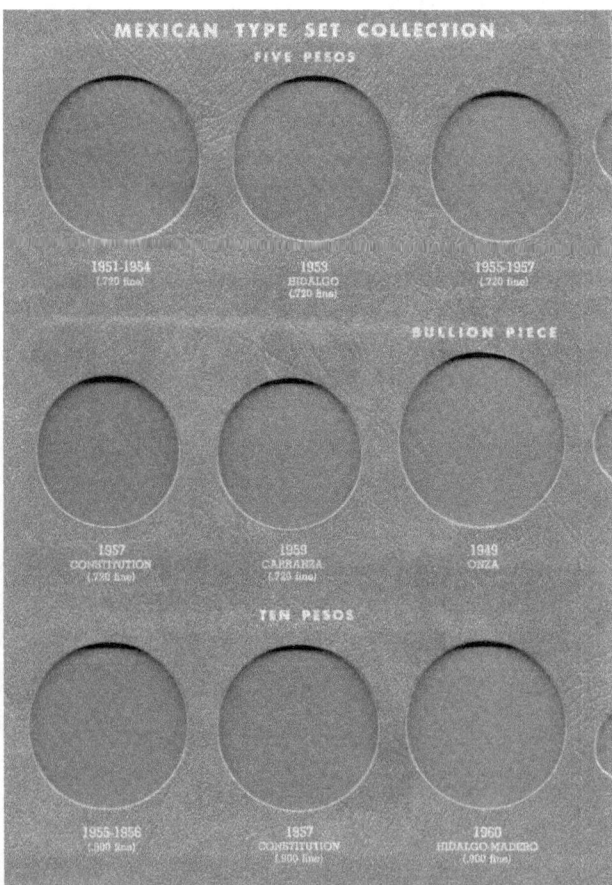

Whitman album 9524 had ports for Mexican five and ten peso coins issued in the 1950s, as well as a port for the "onza" struck in 1949.

Newfoundland

Newfoundland, the oldest British colony in North America, joined the Canadian Confederation in 1949. Prior to that time, Newfoundland was a separate colony with its own currency. The colony issued decimal coins beginning in 1865. The last Newfoundland coins were dated 1947.

Whitman issued five folders and an album to hold the coins issued by Newfoundland. The folders also contain ports for the coins issued by the other Maritime Provinces.

Whitman folders:		*Price guide:*
9074	Cents and half cents of British North America	$3 - $5
	The above folder contains ports for the half cent and one cent coins of Nova Scotia, and the one cent coins of New Brunswick and Prince Edward Island. There is also a knock-out port for the half cent coin of New Brunswick, which was struck in error.	
9075	Newfoundland five cents 1865-1947	$3 - $5
	The above folder includes ports for the five, ten, and twenty cent coins issued by New Brunswick in 1862 and 1864.	
9076	Newfoundland ten cents 1865-1947	$3 - $5
9077	Newfoundland twenty and twenty-five cents 1865-1919	$3 - $5
9078	Newfoundland fifty cents 1870-1919	$4 - $6
9088	Newfoundland type coin collection	$8 - $10

Whitman album:		*Price guide:*
9514	Newfoundland type set	$10 - $15

See also BRITISH NORTH AMERICA.

NEWFOUNDLAND –

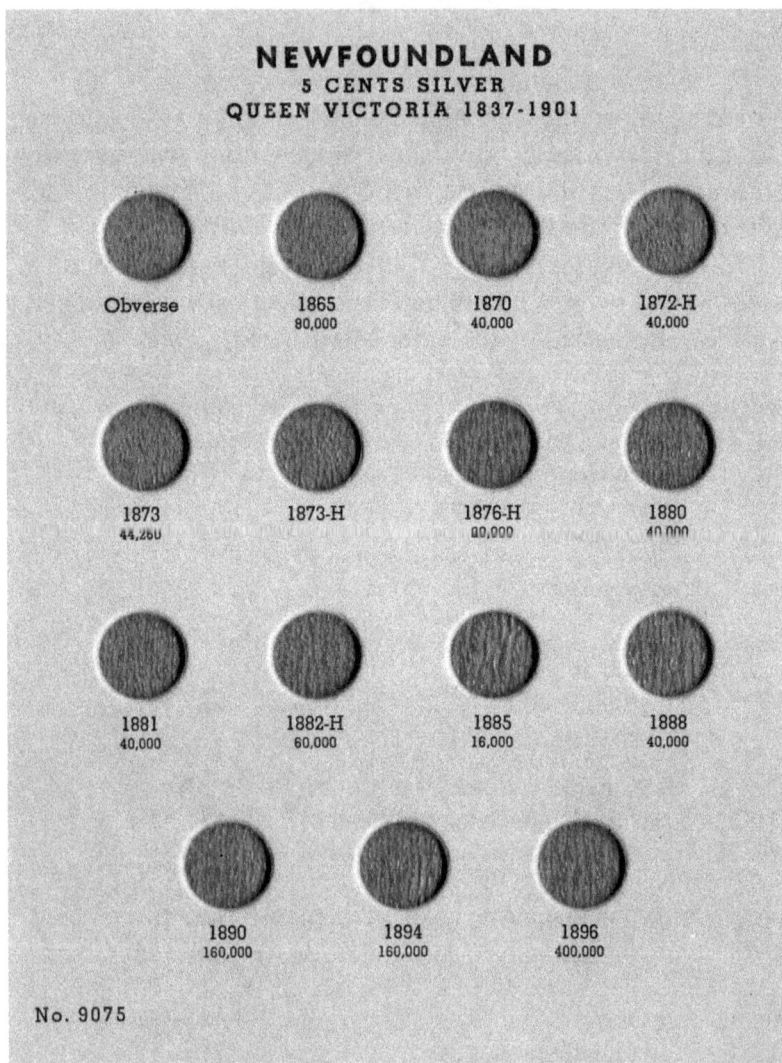

NEWFOUNDLAND
5 CENTS SILVER
QUEEN VICTORIA 1837-1901

Obverse	1865 80,000	1870 40,000	1872-H 40,000
1873 44,260	1873-H	1876-H 00,000	1880 40,000
1881 40,000	1882-H 60,000	1885 16,000	1888 40,000
	1890 160,000	1894 160,000	1896 400,000

No. 9075

Newfoundland five cent coins could be collected in Whitman folder 9075. It contained openings for all of the silver five cent coins issued by Newfoundland, as well as the silver coins issued by New Brunswick.

New Guinea

The large island of New Guinea is located north of Australia. In the scramble for colonies in the mid-1880s, the island was divided among the Netherlands, Germany, and Great Britain. The British section, also called Papua, was turned over to Australia in 1906. During the First World War, Australian troops invaded and occupied German New Guinea. After the war, German New Guinea was given to Australia. The two territories – Papua and German New Guinea – were united to form the Territory of New Guinea. The Australians kept the territory until 1975, when it became an independent country: Papua New Guinea.

Special coinage for New Guinea was first struck in 1929. The issue consisted of halfpennies and pennies. The mintage was extremely low, and the coins command hefty prices. A new issue of coins was produced in the 1930s and continued into the next decade. That series included penny, threepence, sixpence, and shilling pieces. All Territory of New Guinea coins were struck with a central hole, a feature unique within the British Empire coinage. Excluding the 1929 dated coins, the entire series of New Guinea issues totaled eleven coins.

A two-page folder for New Guinea coins was produced by Dansco. There are thirteen ports in the folder, but the ones for the 1929-dated coins were plugged. Despite the title on the cover, *New Guinea type coins*, the folder actually held all dates of all coins struck for the territory.

Dansco folder: *Price guide:*
360   New Guinea type $8 - $10

43

NEW GUINEA –

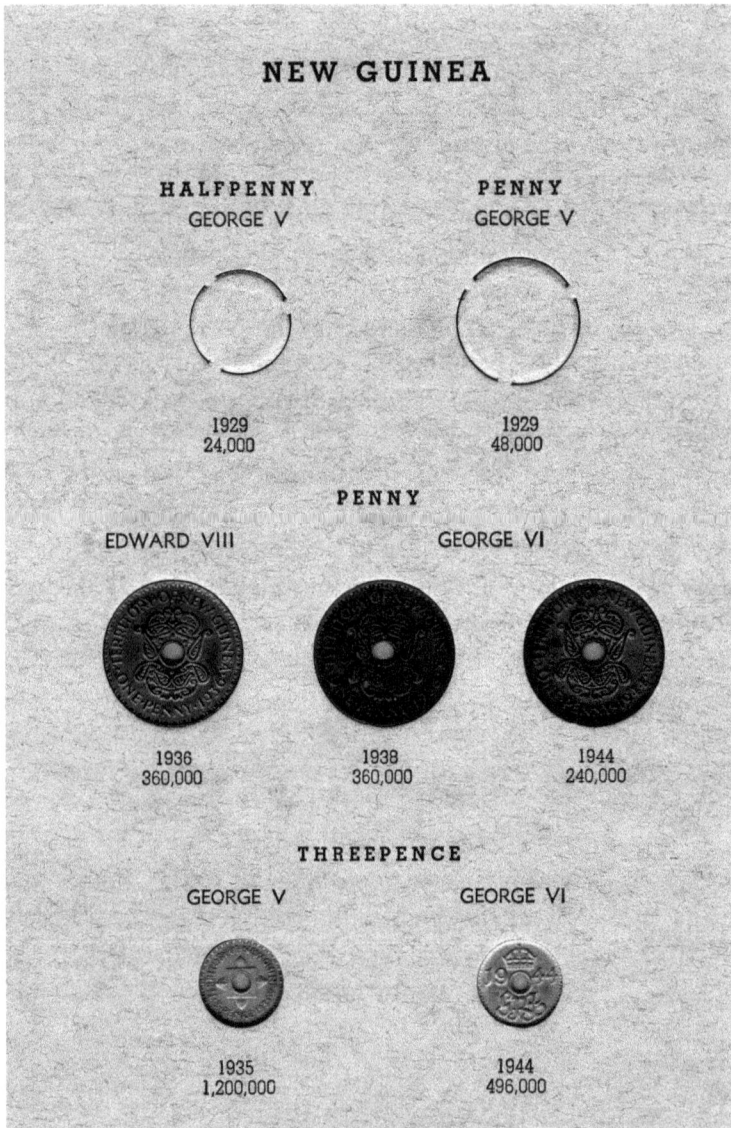

Dansco produced a two-page folder for the coins of the Territory of New Guinea. The ports for the coins of King George V remain plugged, due to the rarity of the coins.

New Zealand

The first coins issued by New Zealand appeared in 1933, when threepences, sixpences, shillings, florins, and half crowns were struck. Bronze halfpennies and pennies did not arrive until 1940. Crowns were struck in 1935, 1949, and 1953. The pounds, shillings, and pence currency system was retained until 1967, when the country switched to a decimal system.

Folders for New Zealand's pre-decimal coinage were produced by Dansco and two New Zealand firms, John Bertrand and Warrior.

Bertrand Folders

The Bertrand folders were consisted of three pages and a leaf of paper, and measured 6 by 7½ inches when closed. They were almost identical in size, design, and style to the Whitman blue folders. The overleaf described the history and design of the coins contained in the folder. Ports were labeled by date and included the mintage for each coin, and ports for obverses were included. Extra ports were labeled "variety." Some albums have ports that bear the date 1966. New Zealand did not issue coins dated 1966; obviously these folders were in production prior to that date. The folders were covered in various colors of textured paper, and the titles were printed silver. The type set folder included a cardboard reproduction of the Centennial half crown and the Waitangi crown. These folders are offered for sale occasionally on internet

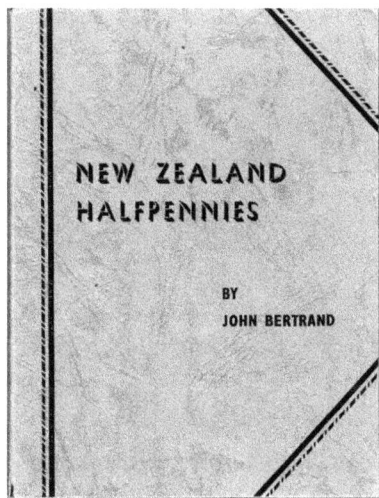

NEW ZEALAND
HALFPENNIES

BY
JOHN BERTRAND

NEW ZEALAND –

auction sites based in New Zealand. I have even seen a florin folder relabeled to house a collection of New Zealand twenty cent pieces!

Bertrand folders:	*Price guide:*
Halfpennies 1940-1965	$3 - $6
Pennies 1940-1965	$3 - $6
Threepences 1933-1965	$3 - $6
Sixpences 1933-1965	$3 - $6
Shillings 1933-1965	$4 - $7
Florins 1933-1965	$3 - $6
Half Crowns 1933-1965	$3 - $6
Type set 1933-1965	$4 - $7

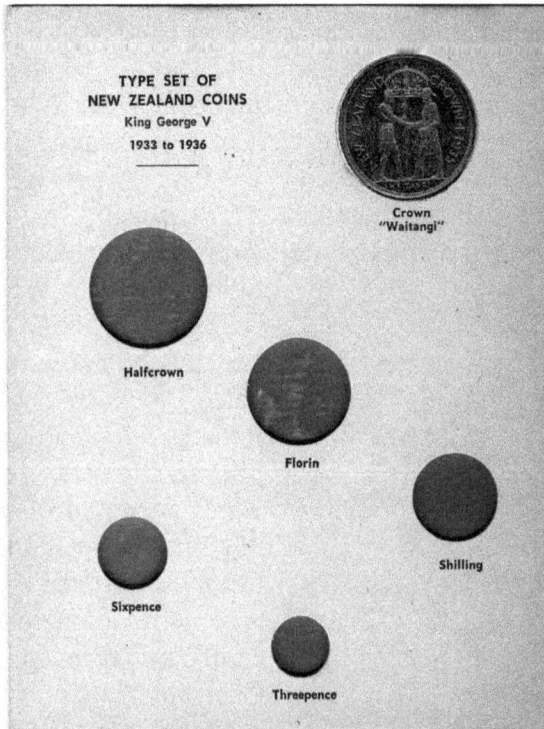

TYPE SET OF
NEW ZEALAND COINS
King George V
1933 to 1936

Crown
"Waitangi"

Halfcrown

Florin

Sixpence

Shilling

Threepence

The Bertrand New Zealand type set folder had a cardboard facsimile of the rare Waitangi crown.

NEW ZEALAND –

Dansco Folders

The Dansco folders were produced in the usual 6½ by 9¼ inch format with brown leatherette covers. The covers and spine were labeled in gold. Each folder had ports for two denominations and consisted of four pages. The half crown and crown folder had three pages.

Dansco folders:		*Price guide:*
440	Halfpenny and penny	$6 - $10
442	Threepence and sixpence	$6 - $10
443	Shilling and Florin	$6 - $10
444	Half crown and crown	$8 - $12
447	New Zealand Type	$8 - $12

A page from Dansco folder 443 showing a collection of New Zealand shillings from the reigns of King George VI and Queen Elizabeth II. An extra port accommodates a ten cent coin of 1967, the decimal equivalent of a shilling.

NEW ZEALAND –

Warrior Folders
A series of folders entitled *Warrior Coin Album* was produced in the mid-1960s. Measuring 6½ by 9½ inches, the folders had openings labeled with the date and mintage of each coin. An extra port was included to show the obverse of the coin for each monarch, though no accommodation was made for the second obverse of King George VI issued from 1948 to 1952. Some folders contained information on coin collecting and information about the composition of New Zealand coins.

Warrior folders:	*Price guide:*
Halfpennies	not seen
Pennies	not seen
Threepences	not seen
Sixpences	$4 - $7
Shillings	$4 - $7
Florins	not seen

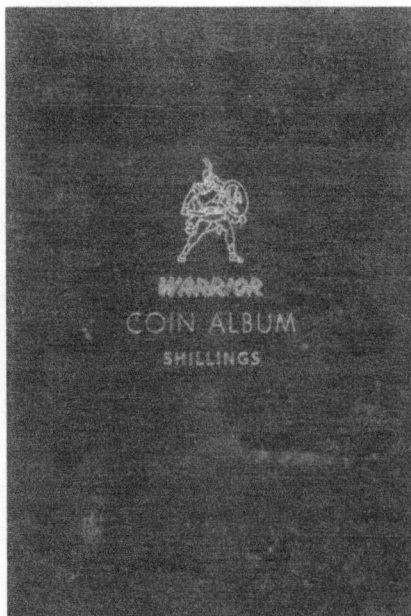

The cover of the Warrior folder for New Zealand shillings.

Nicaragua

Nicaragua declared its independence from Spain in 1821, and became an independent republic in 1838. The country began to issue coins in 1878. At that time the main unit of currency was the *peso*, divided into 100 *centavos*. This system was continued until 1912, when the *cordoba* was adopted as the main unit of currency. It was also divided into 100 centavos.

In the early 1960s Dansco produced several folders for the coinage of various Latin American countries. In the early 1990s I had the opportunity to purchase a Nicaragua folder for a few dollars, but passed. That was the only example I have ever seen offered for sale.

Dansco folder
235   Nicaragua type coins, 1878-

Price guide:
$6 - $15

Norway

Norway joined the Scandinavian Monetary Union in 1875, two years after its formation by Denmark and Sweden. Norway began to issue coins denominated in *kroner* and *øre* in 1875. With a few exceptions, the size and composition of Norwegian coinage changed little during the next hundred years. The coinage system was revamped in the mid-1990s. The 10 øre coin ceased to be issued, and the diameters of the 50 øre, one krone, and five kroner coins were reduced.

Frovin Sieg, who produced coin folders for Danish coins, published a similar series of folders for the Norwegian coinage. The folders measured 6⅝ by 8¾ inches, and were covered in a red, faux leather fabric. The covers were lettered in gold. Each album included a page that contained black-and-white photographs of each type of coin housed in the album, along with a brief description of the coins. The folders did not carry stock numbers, but were organized by denomination. Originally priced at 35-45 kroner per album, they are occasionally seen on Norwegian internet auction sites. No folders were produced for the new series of Norwegian coins introduced in the 1990s.

NORWAY –

Sieg folder:	Price Guide:
1 øre 1876-1972	$7 - $10
2 øre 1876-1972	$7 - $10
5 øre 1875-1970	$7 - $10
5 øre 1971-	$5 - $7

The 5 øre coin was last issued in 1982.

10 øre 1874-1985	$7 - $10
10 øre blank	$5 - $7

*The 10 øre coin was last issued in 1991.
This folder could be used to house the
coins dated after 1986.*

25 øre 1876-1982	$7 - $10
50 øre 1874-1987	$7 - $10
50 øre blank	$5 - $7

*The last 50 øre coins that will fit in this
album were issued in 1996. This folder
could be used to house the coins dated
after 1987.*

1 krone 1875-1970	$7 - $10
1 krone 1971-	$5 - $7

*The last 1 krone coins that will fit in this
album were issued in 1996.*

2 kroner 1878-1917 with gold coins 1874-1910	$15 - $20
2 kroner 1878-1917 with 5 kroner 1963-1977	$15 - $20
5 kroner, no dates	$5 - $7
10 kroner 1983-	$7 - $10

*This album can hold current the 10
kroner coins of King Harald V.*

Commemorative and gold coins	$15 - $20

NORWAY –

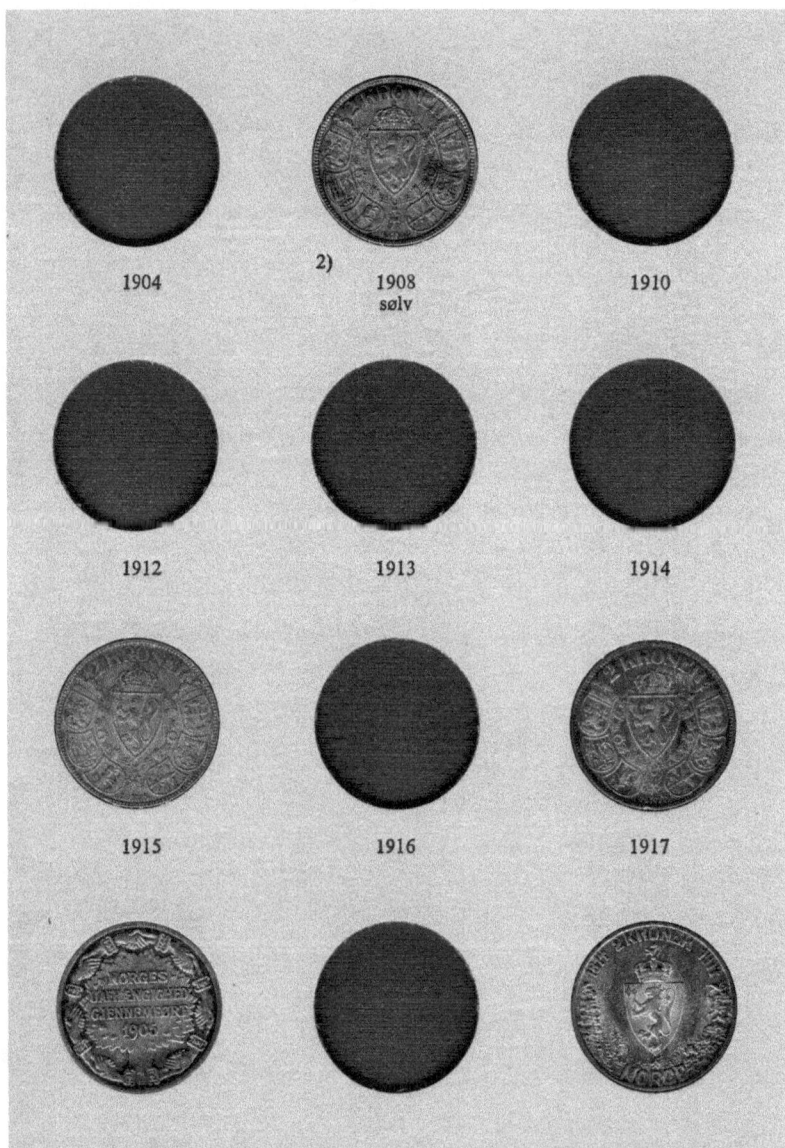

This is the second page of the Sieg folder for Norwegian two kroner coins. The free ports at the bottom have been used to house two Norwegian commemoratives: the 1905 independence issue and the 1914 constitution centennial.

Panama

The Republic of Panama became independent of Colombia in 1903 and issued its first coins the following year. There has been a close economic relationship between Panama and the United States; the Panamanian *Balboa* is equivalent in value to the United States dollar.

Folders and albums for Panamanian coins were produced by Dansco and Whitman.

Dansco folder: *Price guide:*
452   Panama type coins $10 - $20
          This folder can hold coins struck
          from 1904 to the series of coins
          issued in the 1960s.

Whitman Album: *Price Guide:*
9518   Type coins, 1904-1960s $12 - $30

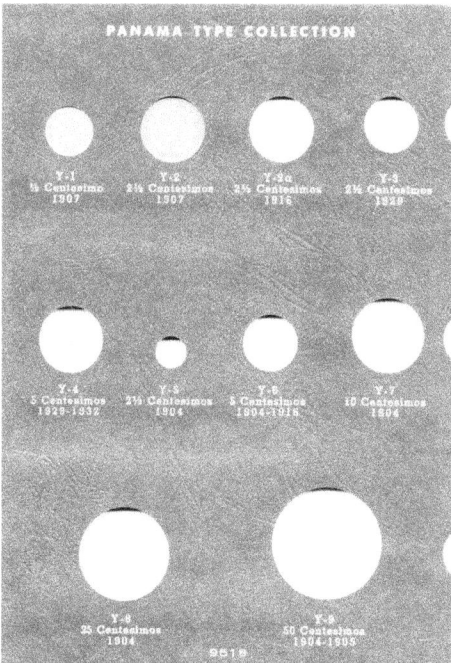

The first page of Whitman album 9518 for the type coins of Panama.

53

Philippines

The Philippine Islands, located in the Pacific Ocean, were colonized by the Spanish. The islands became a possession of the United States after the Spanish-American War. Spanish colonial coinage was struck between 1864 and 1897; the United States issued a special Philippine coinage between 1903 and 1945. The Philippines became an independent republic in 1946.

Whitman manufactured an album for a type set of Philippine coins. One page of the album was dedicated to the Spanish colonial issues, and has space for coins issued during the reigns of Queen Isabella II and King Alfonso XII. Two pages have ports for the coinage issued by the United States for the Philippines. The last page has openings for coins of the republic issued between 1947 and 1961.

Whitman album: *Price guide:*
9526   Type coins, 1864-1961 $10 - $20

PHILIPPINES –

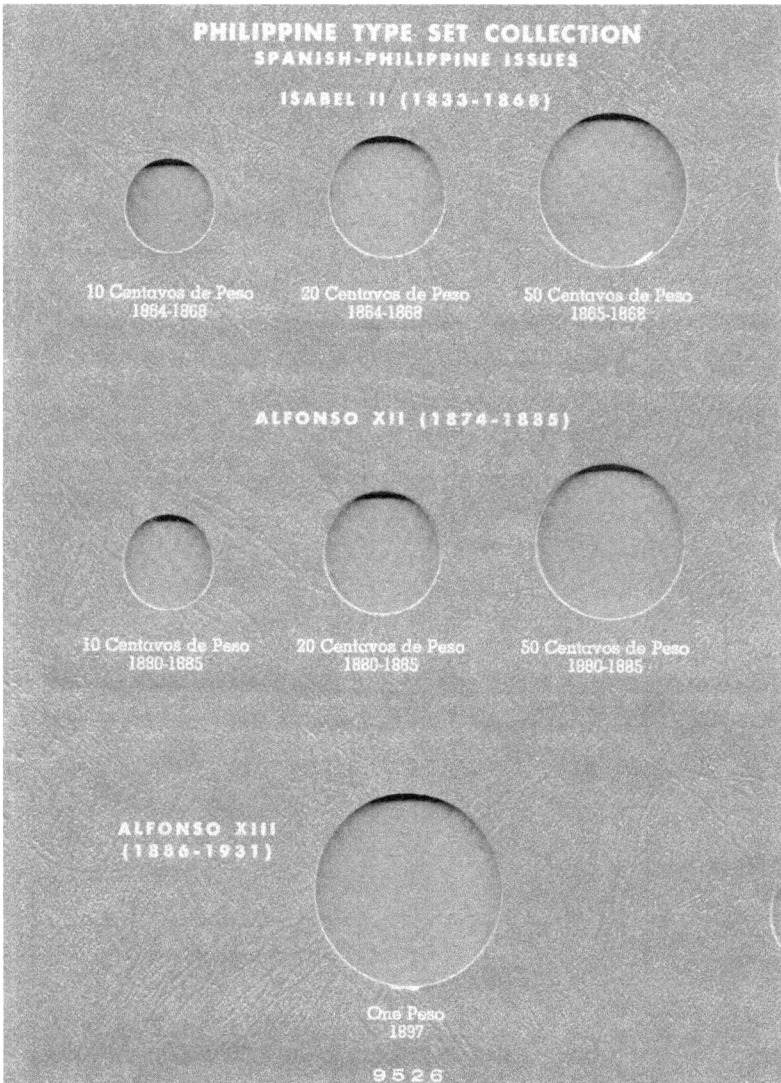

The Whitman album for Philippine type coins had a page for the Philippine colonial coinage issued by Spain.

Sweden

The modern coinage of Sweden dates from 1873, when the country joined with Denmark in a monetary union. Sweden adopted the *krona* as the main currency unit, which was divided into 100 *öre*.

Weilands of Uppsala, Sweden printed a series of coin folders in the 1960s for the Swedish coinage; these were marketed by Scandia. The folders could house the coins struck for King Oscar II, King Gustav V, and King Gustav VI Adolf. The folders were blue with silver lettering and measured 5⅝ x 7⅞ inches. Folders could have two or three pages. Some folders contained extra ports for varieties; these could also be used to display obverse coins. Scandia folders were numbered, with each folder housing the coins of one denomination by monarch.

Scandia folders had a few quirks not seen in the folders produced by other countries. In some cases, joint albums were printed. For example, folder numbers three and six were combined so that the one öre and two öre coins of King Gustav VI Adolf were housed in the same folder. The backs of some folders have price charts for the harder-to-find coins contained in that particular folder. Some retailers had their names and addresses printed on the backs of the folders as well.

Scandia folders are seen occasionally on Swedish auction websites. Bids for individual folders have topped $15.

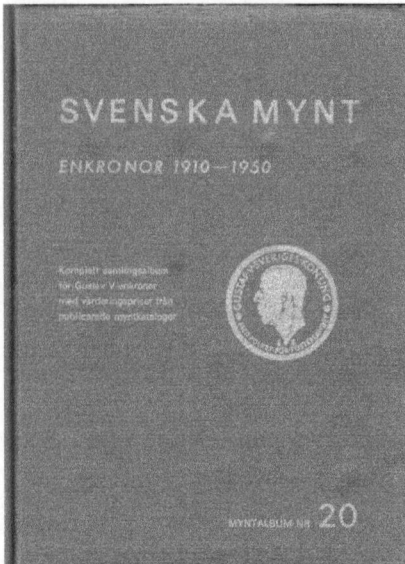

SWEDEN –

Scandia folder:		Price Guide:
1	1 öre 1874-1907	$8 - $15
2	1 öre 1909-1950	$5 - $15
3	1 öre 1952-	$5 - $15
4	2 öre 1874-1907	$8 - $15
5	2 öre 1909-1950	$5 - $15
6	2 öre 1952-	$5 - $15
7	5 öre 1874-1907	$8 - $15
8	5 öre 1909-1950	$5 - $15
9	5 öre 1952-	$5 - $15
10	10 öre 1874-1907	$8 - $15
11	10 öre 1909-1950	$5 - $15
12	10 öre 1952-	$5 - $15
13	25 öre 1874-1907	$8 - $15
14	25 öre 1910-1950	$5 - $15
15	25 öre 1952-	$5 - $15
16	50 öre 1875-1907	$8 - $15
17	50 öre 1909-1952	$5 - $15
18	50 öre 1952-	$5 - $15
19	1 krona 1875-1907	$8 - $15
20	1 krona 1910-1950	$5 - $15
21	1 krona 1952-	$5 - $15
22	2 kronor 1876-1907	$8 - $15
23	2 kronor 1910-1950	$5 - $15
24	2 kronor 1952-	$5 - $15
25	5 kronor / Commemoratives	$10 - $15

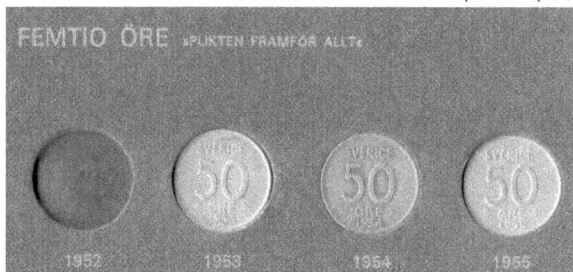

Scandia folder 18, for the 50 öre coins of Gustav IV Adolf.

Switzerland

The Swiss Confederation, though founded in 1291, did not issue a national coinage until 1850. The Constitution of 1848 gave the Swiss federal government the sole right to issue coins. Up to that time each canton issued its own coinage. Modern Swiss circulating coins have been issued with the same basic design since the 1870s.

A folder and an album were produced for Swiss coins by Dansco. A fine series of albums was produced in Switzerland by Moneta.

Dansco

Dansco produced a folder for Swiss type coins, and also an album as part of the *Continental Line* of albums. Both are rarely seen.

Dansco folder: *Price guide:*
500   Swiss Confederation type set   not seen

Continental Line album: *Price guide:*
Swiss type   not seen

SWITZERLAND –

Moneta Albums

These albums, which are not unlike the Whitman albums, were produced in the late 1960s through the early 1980s. The Moneta albums measured approximately 7 by 8¾ inches and had dark green leatherette covers. The pages were covered in the same material, and were bound into the spine. Ports for coins were arranged vertically in two columns, with the acetate sleeves being loaded from the top. Ports were labeled in gold with the date; the spine was also stamped in gold with the denomination near the top of the spine. A representation of the Swiss cross on a shield was stamped in gold at the bottom of the spine.

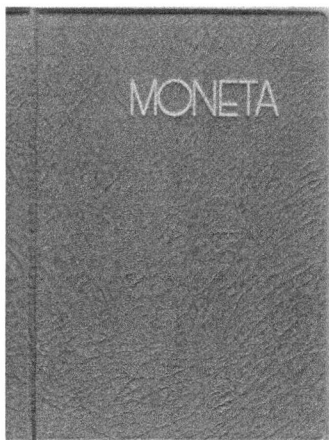

Moneta albums:	*Price guide:*
One rappen 1850-	$10 - $20
Two rappen 1850-	not seen
Five rappen 1850-	$10 - $20
Ten rappen 1850-	$10 - $20
Twenty rappen 1850-	$10 - $20
Half franc 1850-	$10 - $20
One franc 1850-	$10 - $20
Two francs 1850-	$10 - $20
Five francs 1850-1928	$12 - $25
Five francs 1931-	not seen
Gold coins 1883-1925	$12 - $25

59

SWITZERLAND –

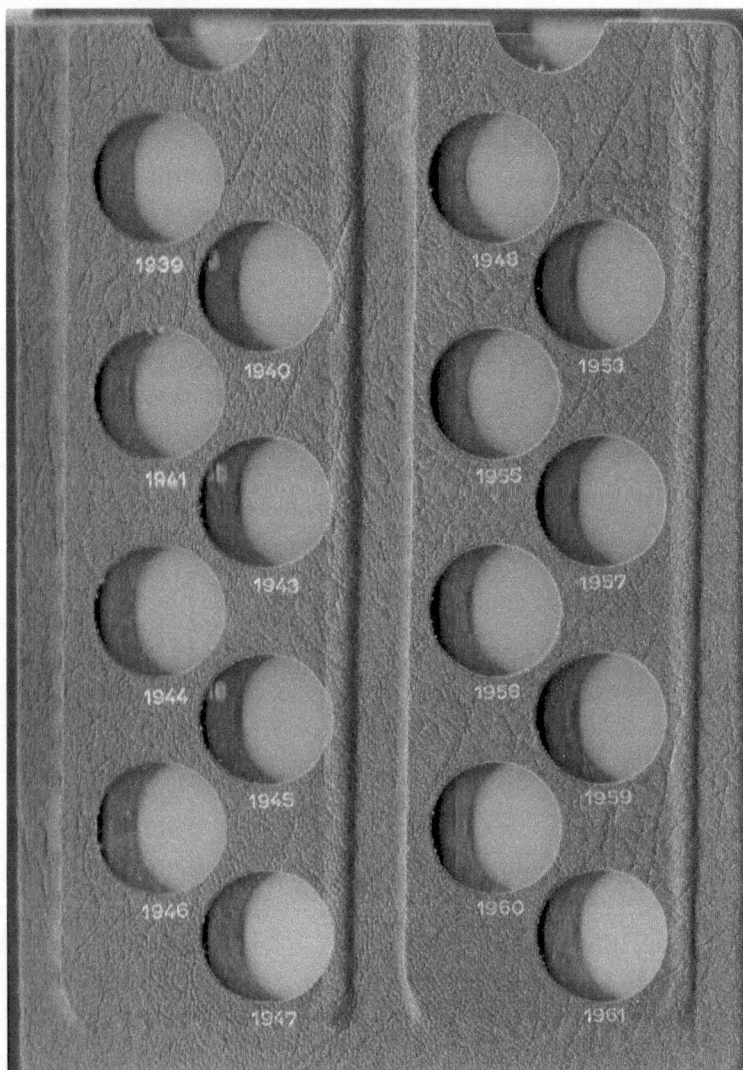

**A page from the two franc album produced by Moneta,
showing the unusual vertical arrangement of the ports.**

United States

Despite the fact that the United States gained its independence in 1776, the country did not issue its own coins until 1792. These early issues had extremely small mintages, and foreign coins continued to circulate in the United States to augment the coinage. Foreign coins were outlawed in 1857, when the mints were able to meet the demand for coins.

Given the large number of coin collectors in the United States, it is not surprising that Dansco and Whitman found success in manufacturing folders and albums to house United States coins. The variety of albums and folders suggests that there was a strong demand for this method of housing a collection.

Dansco folders

Dansco produced a large series of folders to hold Unites States coins. An older series of folders, made with gray pages and covers, was produced in the 1950s. The folders listed below are of the more modern type. They were covered in brown leatherette and consisted of two or more fold-out pages.

Dansco folders:		*Price guide:*
90	Indian penny	$4 - $6
100	Lincoln penny 1909-	$3 - $5
101	Lincoln penny 1909-1929	$3 - $5
102	Lincoln penny 1930-1950	$3 - $5
103	Lincoln penny 1951-	$3 - $5
110	Nickel 1883-	$4 - $6
111	Liberty nickel 1883-1913	$3 - $5
112	Buffalo nickel 1913-1938	$3 - $5
113	Jefferson nickel 1938-	$3 - $5
120	Dime 1892-	$4 - $6
121	Liberty dime 1892-1916	$3 - $5
122	Mercury dime 1916-1945	$3 - $5

UNITED STATES –

123	Roosevelt dime 1946-	$3 - $5
130	Liberty head quarter 1892-1916	$3 - $5
135	Standing liberty quarter 1916-1930	$3 - $5
140	Washington quarter 1932-	$3 - $5
150	Liberty head half 1892-1915	$3 - $5
160	Liberty standing half 1916-1947	$3 - $5
165	Franklin half dollar 1948-1963	$3 - $5
157	General half	$4 - $6
170	Silver dollars 1878-1890	$3 - $5
180	Silver dollars 1891-1921	$3 - $5
190	Silver dollars 1921-1935	$3 - $5
80	General United States coins	$4 - $6

*This folder had five pages; one
page each for penny, nickel,
dime, quarter, and half dollar.*

Whitman Folders

The largest variety of folders for United States coins
was produced by Whitman. All of the Whitman folders were
labeled with a stock number, and this can aid in locating a
particular title. Unfortunately, Whitman reused some of the
stock numbers in recent years. For example, the folder for
Lincoln cents starting 1975 bore the stock number 9033,
which was used for the first Seated liberty quarter folder. This
list below contains the familiar blue folders manufactured up
to the early 1970s; some of the folders continue to be printed
up to the present time.

Whitman folders:		*Price guide:*
9022	Half cent 1793-1857	$7 - $10
9001	Large cent 1793-1825	$7 - $10
9002	Large cent 1826-1857	$7 - $10
9003	Indian Eagle cents 1857-1909	$3 - $5
9004	Lincoln cents 1909-1940	$3 - $5
9030	Lincoln cent 1941-	$3 - $5

UNITED STATES –

9000	Lincoln Memorial 1959-	$3 - $5
9100	Cents, one-a-year, 1909-	$4 - $6
9041	Cents, blank	$4 - $6
9024	Two cent & nickel three cent 1864-1889	$7 - $10
9023	Three cent silver 1851-1873	$7 - $10
9005	Half dime 1794-1873	$7 - $10
9006	Shield type nickel 1866-1883	$4 - $6
9007	Liberty head nickel 1883-1912	$3 - $5
9008	Buffalo nickel 1913-1938	$3 - $5
9009	Jefferson nickel 1938-1961	$3 - $5
9102	Nickels, one-a-year, 1913-	$4 - $6
9042	Nickels, blank	$4 - $6
9010	Bust type dime 1796-1837	$7 - $10
9011	Liberty seated dime 1837-1862	$7 - $10
9012	Liberty seated dime 1863-1891	$7 - $10
9013	Barber dime 1892-1916	$4 - $6
9014	Mercury head dime 1916-1945	$3 - $5
9029	Roosevelt dime 1946-	$3 - $5
9103	Dimes, one-a-year, 1916-	$4 - $6
9043	Dimes, blank	$4 - $6
9033	Liberty seated quarter 1838-1865	$7 - $10
9034	Liberty seated quarter 1866-1891	$7 - $10
9015	Barber quarter 1892-1905	$7 - $10
9016	Barber quarter 1906-1916	$7 - $10
9017	Liberty Standing quarter 1916-1930	$4 - $6
9018	Washington head quarter 1932-1945	$3 - $5
9031	Washington head quarter 1946-1959	$3 - $5
9040	Washington head quarter 1960-	$3 - $5
9104	Quarters, one-a-year, 1916-	$4 - $6
9044	Quarters, blank	$4 - $6
9035	Liberty seated half 1839-1850	$7 - $10
9036	Liberty seated half 1851-1862	$7 - $10
9037	Liberty seated half 1862-1873	$7 - $10
9038	Liberty seated half 1873-1891	$7 - $10
9019	Barber half 1892-1903	$7 - $10

UNITED STATES –

9020	Barber half 1904-1916	$7 - $10
9021	Liberty standing half 1916-1936	$4 - $6
9027	Liberty standing half 1937-1947	$4 - $6
9032	Franklin half 1948-1963	$3 - $5
9699	Kennedy half 1964-	$3 - $5
9045	Halves, blank	$4 - $6
9082	Morgan dollar 1878-1883	$7 - $10
9083	Morgan dollar 1884-1890	$7 - $10
9084	Morgan dollar 1891-1897	$7 - $10
9085	Morgan dollar 1898-1921	$7 - $10
9028	Peace dollars 1921-1935	$4 - $6
9025	Dollars blank	$4 - $6
9026A	Type coins, small denominations	$4 - $6
9026B	Type coins, large denominations	$4 - $6
9046	Twentieth century type coins	$4 - $6

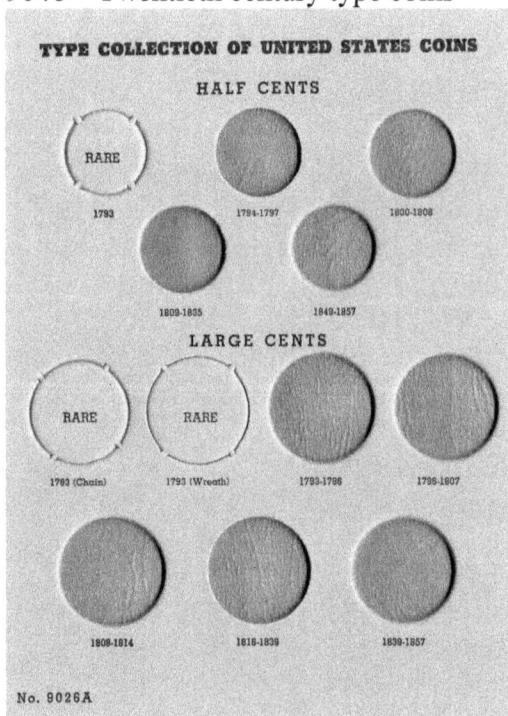

The first page of Whitman folder 9026A, for type coins of the United States. Ports for the early types retained the plugs.

UNITED STATES –

Whitman albums

Though not as extensive in variety as the series of folders, Whitman produced a large number of albums for United States coins.

Whitman album:		*Price guide:*
9400	Half cents 1793-1857	$10 - $20
9401	Large cents 1793-1857	$10 - $20
9402	Indian cents 1856-1909	$7 - $10
9405	Lincoln cents 1909-1940	$7 - $10
9406	Lincoln cents 1941-	$7 - $10
9441	Cents, blank – 120 ports	$7 - $10
9436	Two cents, three cents, shield five cents and twenty cents	$10 - $20
9411	Liberty seated half dimes 1837-1873	$10 - $20
9407	Liberty nickels 1883-1912	$7 - $10
9408	Buffalo nickels 1913-1938	$7 - $10
9410	Jefferson nickels 1938-1964	$7 - $10
9442	Nickels, blank – 96 ports	$7 - $10
9437	Liberty seated dimes 1837-1891	$10 - $20
9412	Liberty dimes 1892-1916	$10 - $20
9413	Mercury dime 1916-1945	$7 - $10
9414	Roosevelt dime 1946-	$7 - $10
9443	Dimes, plain – 120 ports	$7 - $10
9439	Liberty seated quarters 1838-1865	$10 - $20
9440	Liberty seated quarters 1866-1891	$10 - $20
9416	Liberty quarters 1892-1916	$10 - $20
9417	Liberty standing quarters 1916-1930	$7 - $10
9418	Washington quarters 1932-1964	$7 - $10
9444	Quarters, blank – 84 ports	$7 - $10
9415	Bust half 1807-1839	$20 - $30
9447	Liberty seated half 1839-1863	$20 - $30
9448	Liberty seated half 1864-1891	$20 - $30
9420	Liberty half 1892-1906	$7 - $10
9421	Liberty half 1907-1915	$7 - $10

UNITED STATES –

9423	Liberty walking half 1916-1940	$7 - $10
9424	Liberty walking half 1941-1947	$7 - $10
9425	Franklin half 1948-1963	$7 - $10
9422	Kennedy half 1964-	$7 - $10
9445	Half dollars, blank – 64 openings	$7 - $10
9426	Trade dollars 1873-1883	$20 - $30
9427	Morgan dollars 1878-1886	$10 - $20
9428	Morgan dollars 1887-1896	$10 - $20
9429	Morgan dollars 1897-1921	$10 - $20
9430	Peace dollars 1921-1935	$10 - $20
9446	Dollars, blank – 36 openings	$10 - $20
9434	Type set, half cents to quarters	$15 - $25
9435	Type set, halves and dollars	$15 - $25
9436	Type set, gold coins	$15 - $25
9432	Year sets, blank	not seen
9433	Commemoratives	$15 - $25
9449	Modern mint sets – mint sealed	not seen
9450	Modern proof sets – mint sealed	not seen
9452	Civil War tokens 1861-1865	not seen
9455	Miscellaneous tokens	not seen
9456	Miscellaneous medals	not seen

The World

Whitman produced three albums to house world coins. The *Crowns of the World* album contained thirty-six ports arranged nine on a page. The openings were larger than a United States silver dollar and could accommodate large coins. The openings are approximately forty-two millimeters wide, about the size of a German two-thaler coin.

Each volume of the *Around the World* albums had sixteen ports per page about twenty-nine millimeters in size. Each port has the name of a country printed beneath it; the labels were arranged alphabetically. Each album contained a range of countries: volume I began with Afghanistan and ended with Zambia; volume II started with Albania and finished with Yemen. These two albums were last printed in the 1970s, so the list of coin-issuing countries dates to that era.

Whitman albums:		*Price guide:*
9454	Crowns of the world	$10 - $20
9459	Around-the-world, volume I	$10 - $15
9460	Around-the-world, volume II	$10 - $15

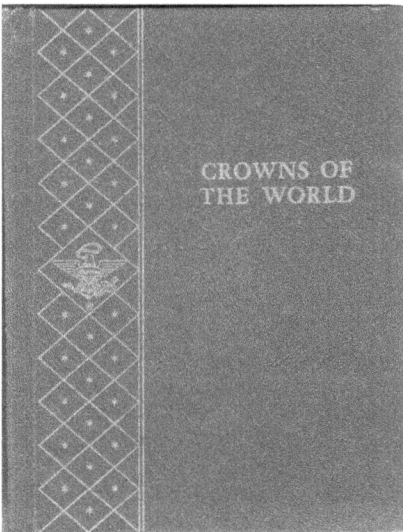

Whitman album 9454 for crowns of the world.

67

Part II

The Possibilities:
Suggestions for using blank folders

For those numismatists who enjoy collecting coins by date, nothing can beat the convenience of a coin folder. A series of coins in a particular denomination can be housed in a small space, and open ports remain for future acquisitions. The blank folder albums listed in Part I, which have unlabeled ports, can be used to house coins of many other countries. In this section of the book, I list possible collections that can be housed in blank Whitman folders. While Dansco did produce some blank folders, Whitman produced a wider and more versatile range of coin folders and albums.

Australia

Although Dansco has produced new folders to house
the decimal coins issued by Australia since 1966, it would be
possible to use blank Whitman folders to house collections of
Australian five cent, ten cent, and twenty cent coins. These
three denominations are identical in size to the coins that they
replaced: sixpence, shilling, and florin.

Use this folder:	*To house this collection:*
W-8005	Five cents 1966-
W-8006	Ten cents 1966-
W-8011	Twenty cents 1966-

Bahamas

The Bahama Islands have been a British colony since
the Seventeenth century. British coins were used in the
Bahamas until the mid-1960s, when the nation switched to a
decimal system based on dollars and cents.

Use this folder:	*To house this collection:*
W-9041	One cent 1970-
W-9042	Five cents 1966 -
W-8006	Ten cents 1966-
W-9044	Twenty-five cents 1966-
W-8011	Fifty cents 1966-

A collection of Bahamian ten cent coins in a Whitman folder.

Belgium

Independent since 1830, Belgium issued coins denominated in francs and centimes from 1832 until the advent of the Euro. Belgian coins were struck with either Flemish or French inscriptions, therefore there are two varieties of a coin for any given date. Some of the modern Belgian coinage can be kept in blank Whitman folders:

Use this folder:	*To house this collection:*
W-9042	One franc 1950-1988
W-9044	Five francs 1948-1999
W-8002	Twenty francs 1980-1999

Whitman folder 9044 can accommodate Belgian five franc coins struck over a fifty-year period.

Bermuda

Bermuda was first settled by British colonists in 1612 and has remained British for nearly four hundred years. The colony used British homeland coins until 1970. At that time, Bermuda adopted a decimal system based on dollars and cents.

BERMUDA –

Use this folder:	To house this collection:
W-9041	One cent 1970-
W-9042	Five cents 1970-
W-9043	Ten cents 1970-
W-9044	Twenty-five cents 1970-
W-9045	Fifty cents 1970-

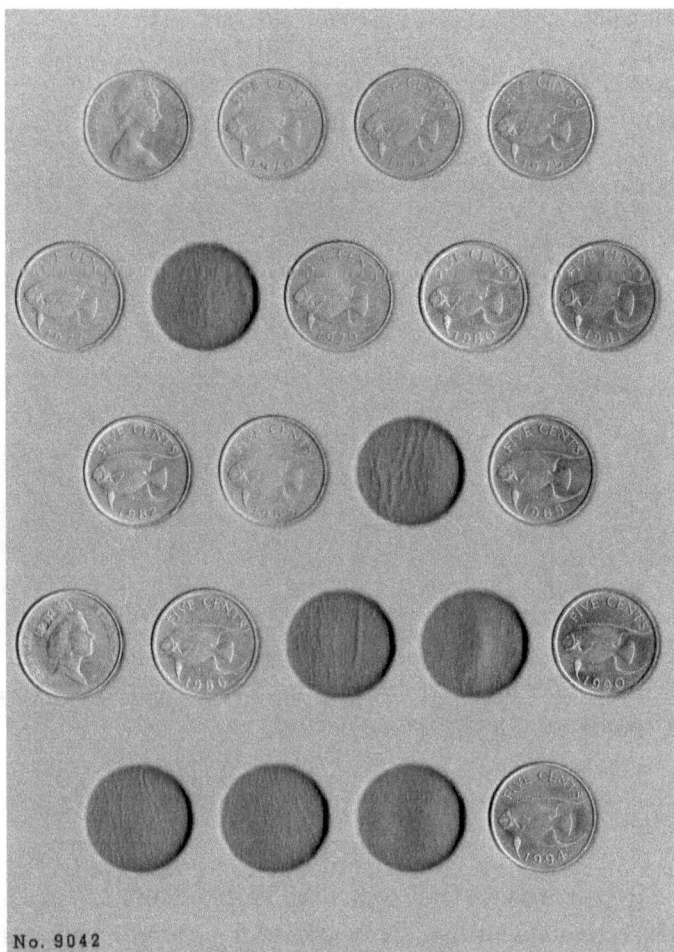

No. 9042

Bermuda began to issue decimal coins in 1970. Above, a collection of five cent coins rests in Whitman folder 9042.

British Caribbean Territories

The numerous British colonies in the Eastern Caribbean were provided coinage through a currency board that was formed in 1950. Decimal coins were issued beginning in 1955.

Use this folder:	*To house this collection:*
W-8001	Half cent 1955-1958
W-8002	Once cent 1955-1965
W-8003	Two cents 1955-1965
W-9042	Five cents 1955-1965
W-9043	Ten cents 1955-1965
W-9079	Twenty-five cents 1955-1965
W-9080	Fifty cents 1955-1965

British West Africa

Four British colonies in Africa – the Gambia, Sierra Leone, the Gold Coast, and Nigeria – were served by the British West Africa Currency Board. The board issued a single coinage for the four territories from 1907 through 1958. Seven denominations were issued: one-tenth pennies, halfpennies, pennies, threepences, sixpences, shillings, and two shillings. It is possible to house most of the British West Africa coinage using blank Whitman folders.

Use this folder:	*To house this collection:*
W-8001	One-tenth pennies 1907-1952
W-8002	Halfpennies 1911-1952
W-8003	Pennies 1907-1956
W-8004	Threepences 1938-1957
W-8005	Sixpences 1913-1952
W-8006	Shillings 1913-1952
W-8011	Two shillings 1913-1952

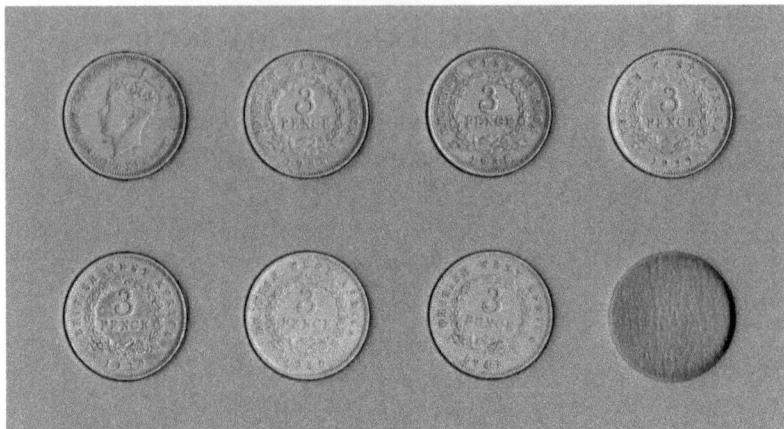

Several threepence coins of British West Africa issued during the reign of King George VI. Threepences can be housed in Whitman folder 8004.

Cyprus

The island of Cyprus, located in the Mediterranean Sea, was occupied by the British in 1878. Coins were issued the following year, where one pound was divided into 180 piastres. In 1955, this system was abandoned and the pound was divided into one thousand mils.

Use this folder:	*To house this collection:*
W-8001	Three mils 1955
W-8002	Five mils 1955-1956
W-8005	Half piastre 1934-1949
W-8006	One piastre 1934-1949
W-8005	Four and a half piastres 1901-1938 & 25 mils 1955
W-8006	Nine piastres 1901-1940, shilling 1947-1949, & fifty mils 1955
W-8011	Eighteen piastres 1901-1940, two shillings 1947-1949, & one hundred mils 1955-1957

Coins from Cyprus: Two nine piastre coins of King George V, a shilling of King George VI, and a fifty mils coin of Queen Elizabeth II share space in a Whitman folder 8006.

Dominican Republic
Since 1937 the Dominican Republic has issued coins on the peso oro standard. The peso was divided into one hundred centavos. The coinage that was struck beginning in 1937 continued into the early 1990s.

Use this folder:	To house this collection:
W-9041	One centavo 1937-
W-9042	Five centavos 1937-
W-9043	Ten centavos 1937-
W-9044	Twenty-five centavos 1937-
W-9045	Half peso, 1937-
W-9025	Peso oro 1939-

East Africa
A common coinage for British Somaliland, Kenya, Uganda, Tanganyika, and Zanzibar was issued by the East Africa Currency Board. First issued in 1922, the East Africa shilling was divided into one hundred cents. Coins were last struck in the mid-1960s. A collection of the lower denomination coins can be housed in blank Whitman folders.

EAST AFRICA –

Use this folder:	To house this collection:
W-8001	One cent 1922-1962
W-8002	Five cents 1921-1964
W-8003	Ten cents 1921-1964
W-9042	Fifty cents 1921-1963

Five cent coins issued by East Africa during the reigns of King George VI and Queen Elizabeth II, all housed on the third page of a Whitman folder 9673.

Falkland Islands

Located off the coast of Argentina, the Falkland Islands have been a British colony since 1833. The islands issued their own coinage beginning in 1974.

Use this folder:	*To house this collection:*
W-8006	Five pence 1974-
W-8011	Ten pence 1974-
W-8004	Twenty pence 1982-
W-9045	Fifty pence 1980-

Fiji

Although Dansco produced a folder for the pre-decimal Fijian coinage, it did not produce anything to hold the new decimal issues. It would be possible to use blank Whitman folders to house collections of Fijian five cent, ten cent, and twenty cent coins. These three denominations are identical in size to the coins that they replaced: sixpence, shilling, and florin.

Use this folder:	*To house this collection:*
W-8005	Five cents 1969-
W-8006	Ten cents 1969-
W-8011	Twenty cents 1969-

France

France has issued coins denominated in francs and centimes since the late 1790s. A currency reform in 1960 introduced one franc coins struck in nickel, with half-franc coins of similar design being introduced five years later. These coins were struck until the advent of the Euro. Franc and half franc coins can be housed in Whitman folders.

FRANCE –

Use this folder:	*To house this collection:*
W-8005	Half franc 1965-
W-9044	Franc 1960-

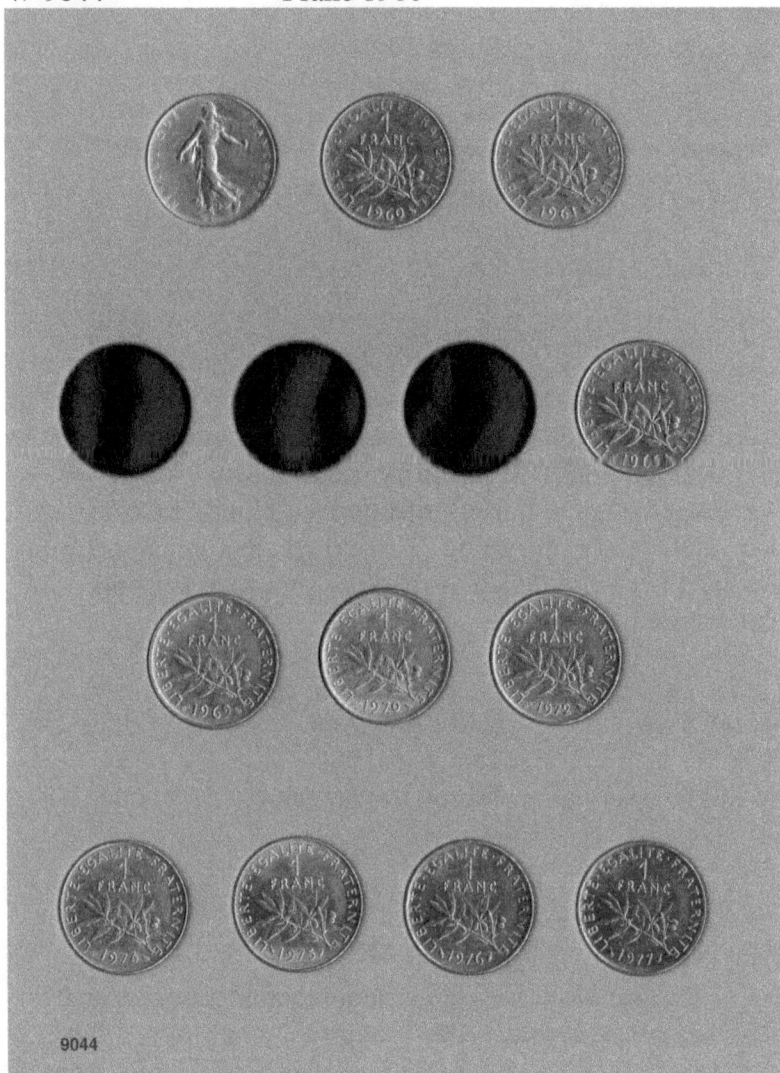

The nickel one franc coins of the Fifth French Republic can be collected in Whitman folder 9044.

Gibraltar

The tiny colony of Gibraltar, located on the southern coast of Spain, issued several tokens denominated in Spanish quartos in the early 1800s. A crown was issued in the late 1960s, and decimal coinage was issued in 1988.

Use this folder:	*To house this collection:*
W-8006	Five pence 1988-
W-8011	Ten pence 1988-
W-8004	Twenty pence 1988-
W-9045	Fifty pence 1988

Great Britain

Britain modernized its coinage beginning in 1816. While Whitman produced a dizzying array of folders and albums for British coins, folders were not produced for collections by date for the coins of Kings George III, George IV, William IV, and Queen Victoria. Therefore, the blank folders could be used to house coins not covered by the existing series of folders. Blank Whitman folders could also be used to collect some of the decimal issues.

Use this folder:	*To house this collection:*
W-8005	Sixpences 1816-1866
W-8005	Sixpences 1867-1901
W-8006	Shillings 1816-1859
W-8006	Shillings 1860-1901
W-8011	Florins 1887-1910
W-8008	Half crowns 1816-1879
W-8008	Half crowns 1880-1910
W-9454	Crowns 1818-1965
W-8006	Five (new) pence 1968-
W-8011	Ten (new) pence 1968-
W-8004	Twenty (new) pence 1982-
W-9045	Fifty (new) pence 1969-

Guernsey

Despite the fact that Whitman (UK) Publishing did produce folders for the coins of Guernsey, I have never seen such folders offered for sale. Blank Whitman folders could be used to house a collection of the "doubles" coinage from this island, as well as some of the decimal coins.

Use this folder:	To house this collection:
W-8002	Four doubles 1864-1956
W-8003	Eight doubles 1864-1959
W-8006	Five (new) pence 1968-
W-8011	Ten (new) pence 1968-
W-8004	Twenty (new) pence 1982-
W-9045	Fifty (new) pence 1969-

India

The British began to issue coins for India portraying the British monarch in 1862. The British issued coins in rupees, annas, and pice. The last Indian coinage that carried an effigy of the British monarch was issued in 1947.

Use this folder:	To house this collection:
W-8005	Half anna 1942-1946
W-9042	One anna 1906-1947
W-8002	Two annas 1918-1945
W-8005	Quarter rupee 1946-1947
W-9044	Half rupee 1904-1947
W-9045	Rupee 1903-1947

Two quarter rupees of India repose in a Whitman folder 8005.

Ireland

Like the United Kingdom, the Republic of Ireland switched to decimal currency in 1971.   Some of the decimal coinage can be housed in folders. Ireland now issues coins denominated in euros and cents.

Use this folder:	*To house this collection:*
W-8006	Five (new) pence 1968-
W-8011	Ten (new) pence 1969-
W-9045	Fifty (new) pence 1970-

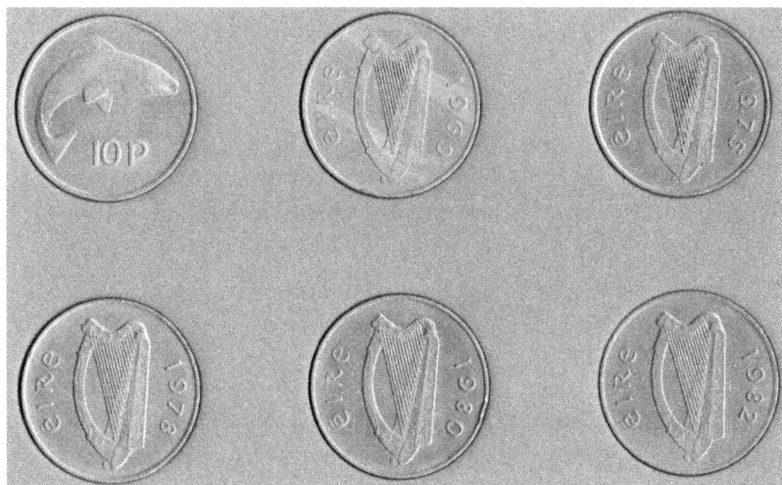

A collection of Irish ten pence coins in Whitman folder 8011.

Isle of Man

The Isle of Man issued modern coinage in 1971, which coincided with the British switching to a decimal system of currency.

Use this folder:	*To house this collection:*
W-8006	Five (new) pence 1971-
W-8011	Ten (new) pence 1971-
W-8004	Twenty (new) pence 1982-
W-9045	Fifty (new) pence 1971-

Jamaica

The island of Jamaica became British in 1670. British coins were first issued in 1825. Special halfpennies and pennies were issued for Jamaica starting in 1869; farthings were struck beginning in 1880. Jamaica continued to issue coins in British currency until the late 1960s, when the island switched to a decimal system.

Use this folder:	*To house this collection:*
W-8001	Farthings 1880-1952
W-8002	Halfpennies 1869-1928
W-8003	Pennies 1869-1928
W-8005	Five cents 1969-
W-8006	Ten cents 1969-
W-8011	Twenty cents 1969-
W-8008	Twenty five cents 1969-

Jersey

Despite the fact that Whitman (UK) Publishing did produce folders for the coins of Jersey, I have never seen such folders offered for sale. Blank Whitman folders could be used to house a collection of fractional shilling coinage from this island, as well as some of the decimal coins.

Use this folder:	*To house this collection:*
W-8002	One twenty-fourth shilling 1877-1947
W-8003	One twelfth shilling 1877-1966
W-8004	One fourth shilling 1957-1966
W-8006	Five (new) pence 1968-
W-8011	Ten (new) pence 1968-
W-8004	Twenty (new) pence 1982-
W-9045	Fifty (new) pence 1969-

Luxembourg

The Grand Duchy of Luxembourg, bordered by
Belgium, France, and Germany, issued a few minor coins in
the 1850s. Coins were issued intermittently thereafter. After
the First World War, Luxembourg entered into a currency
union with Belgium. Modern coins issued in francs were
identical in size and composition to their Belgian equivalents.
Luxembourg now issues coins denominated in euros and cents.

Use this folder:	*To house this collection:*
W-9042	One franc, 1952-1987
W-9044	Five francs, 1962-1999
W-8002	Twenty francs, 1980-1999

Some five franc coins in Whitman folder 9044.

Mauritius

The British acquired Mauritius during the Napoleonic
Wars and was able to keep it under the terms of the Treaty of
Paris in 1814. Located in the Indian Ocean east of Africa,
Mauritius issued minor coins beginning in 1877. Larger
denominations appeared in 1934. The currency unit was the
rupee, which was divided into one hundred cents.

Use this folder:	*To house this collection:*
W-9043	One cent 1877-1975
W-8006	Two cents 1877-1975
W-8008	Five cents 1877-1978
W-8006	Ten cents 1947-1978
W-8005	Quarter rupee 1934-1978
W-9079	Half rupee 1934-1978

New Zealand

To my knowledge, no one has produced folders to house the decimal coins issued by New Zealand since 1967. It would be possible to use blank Whitman folders to house collections of New Zealand five cent, ten cent, and twenty cent coins. These three denominations are identical in size to the coins that they replaced: sixpence, shilling, and florin.

Use this folder:	*To house this collection:*
W-8005	Five cents 1967-
W-8006	Ten cents 1967-
W-8011	Twenty cents 1967-

Panama

Even though both Dansco and Whitman produced specialty folders and albums for a Panamanian type collection, neither produced a full range of folders for a date collection. It would be possible to house a complete date run of modern coins of Panama using blank folders:

Use this folder:	*To house this collection:*
W-9041	One centesimo 1935-
W-9042	Five centesimos 1961-
W-9043	Ten centesimos 1930-
W-9044	Quarter Balboa 1930-
W-9045	Half Balboa 1930-
W-9025	Balboa 1931-

South African Republic
Union of South Africa
Republic of South Africa

The Union of South Africa, founded in 1910 by uniting Cape Colony, the Orange River Colony, Natal, and Transvaal, issued coins beginning in 1923. The coins issued were modeled on the British coinage system, and included eight denominations ranging from farthing to half crown. A crown, or five shilling coin, was produced starting in 1947. South Africa switched to a decimal system of currency in 1961.

Blank Whitman folders can be used to house a collection of South African coins struck from 1923 to 1960. A few of the decimal coins can also be housed in these folders. Sadly, Whitman never produced a blank folder for the small-sized silver threepence coins.

Use this folder:	To house this collection:
W-8001	Farthings 1923-1960
W-8002	Halfpennies 1923-1960
W-8003	Pennies 1923-1960
W-8005	Sixpences 1923-1960
W-8006	Shillings 1923-1960
W-8011	Florins 1923-1960
W-8008	Half crowns 1923-1960
W-9454	Crowns 1947-1959

The South African Republic, founded by Afrikaner farmers in 1852, was incorporated into the British Empire as the colony of Transvaal in 1902. Eight years later, the Transvaal was joined to three neighboring colonies to form the Union of South Africa.

The Republic of South Africa was formed in 1961, when the Union of South Africa left the British Commonwealth. At the same time, the country switched to a decimal system of currency. The main currency unit, the *rand*, was divided into one hundred cents. Some of the initial issues

SOUTH AFRICA –

of decimal coinage were identical in size and composition to the earlier coins.

Collections of the South African Republic and the Republic of South Africa would be small, and could be combined in single folders.

Use this folder:	*To house this collection:*
W-8002	Half cent, 1961-64
W-8003	Pennies 1892-98 / One cent 1961-64
W-8005	Sixpences 1892-97 / five cents 1961-64
W-8006	Shillings 1892-97 / ten cents 1961-1964
W-8011	Florins 1892-97 / twenty cents 1961-64
W-8008	Half crowns 1892-1897

A collection of South Africa 2½ shilling coins from the reign of King George V housed in a Whitman folder 8008.

86

Southern Rhodesia
Federation of Rhodesia and Nyasaland
Rhodesia – Malawi - Zambia

Coins based on the pounds, shillings, and pence standard were first issued for the colony of Southern Rhodesia in 1932. When Southern Rhodesia joined Northern Rhodesia and Nyasaland in a federation in 1953, the coinage reflected the new political entity. Federation coinage began in 1955; when the Federation dissolved in 1963 the coinage ended. Southern Rhodesia, which was called simply Rhodesia, issued coins beginning in 1964. The 1964 coinage was denominated in both shillings/pence and cents, although the decimal system was not adopted until 1970. Collections of coins from these three entities are small and similar denominations can be housed in a single folder:

Use this folder:	To house this collection:
W-9042	Halfpennies 1934-1964
W-8005	Sixpences / five cents 1932-1977
W-8006	Shillings / ten cents 1932-1977
W-8011	Florins / twenty cents 1932-1977
W-8008	Half crowns / twenty-five cents 1932-1975

Nyasaland and Northern Rhodesia left the Federation in 1963 and became, respectively, the independent nations of Malawi and Zambia. Each issued transition coinage in the 1960s before switching to decimal systems.

Use this folder:	To house this collection:
W-8005	Malawi sixpence 1964-67
	Zambia sixpence 1964-66
W-8006	Malawi shillings 1964-68
	Zambia shillings 1964-66
W-8011	Malawi florin 1964
	Zambia florins 1964-66
W-8008	Malawi half crown 1964

SOUTHERN RHODESIA –

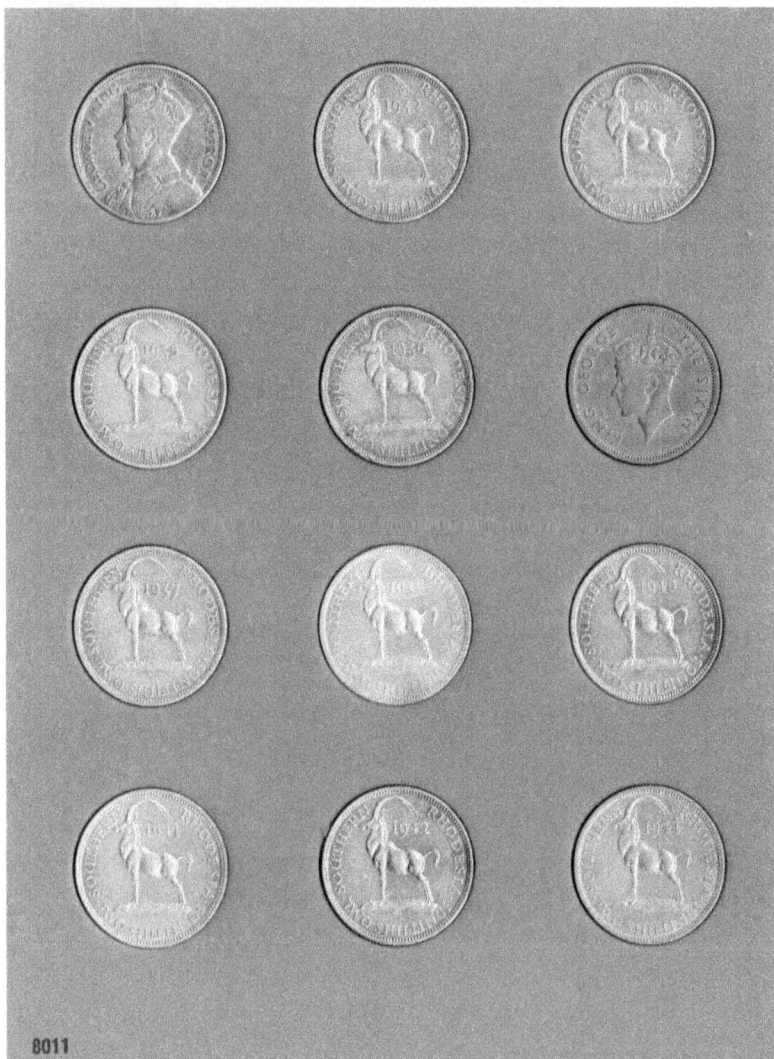

Whitman folder 8011 can house a complete collection of two shilling coins issued by Southern Rhodesia, Rhodesia and Nyasaland, Rhodesia, Malawi, and Zambia.

Part III

The Stock Numbers

Dansco and Whitman produced a large number of coin folders and albums, so it was a logical step to assign stock numbers to their products. In this section I have listed the albums in numerical order by stock number as a cross-reference. By examining the lists one can see that both companies had certain patterns to their stock numbering systems.

Dansco folders
Folders produced by Dansco have two or three digits.

Dansco folders:
80	General United States coins
90	Indian penny
100	Lincoln penny 1909-
101	Lincoln penny 1909-1929
102	Lincoln penny 1930-1050
103	Lincoln penny 1951-
110	Nickel 1883-
111	Liberty nickel 1883-1913
112	Buffalo nickel 1913-1938
113	Jefferson nickel 1938-
120	Dime 1892-

DANSCO FOLDERS –

121   Liberty dime 1892-1916
122   Mercury dime 1916-1945
123   Roosevelt dime 1946-
130   Liberty head quarter 1892-1916
135   Standing liberty quarter 1916-1930
140   Washington quarter 1932-
150   Liberty head half 1892-1915
160   Liberty standing half 1916-1947
165   Franklin half dollar 1948-1963
157   General half
170   Silver dollars 1878-1890
180   Silver dollars 1891-1921
190   Silver dollars 1921-1935

200   Canadian small cents
201   Canadian five cents
202   Canadian ten cents
203   Canadian twenty-five cents 1858-1952

220   Mexican type set 1905-
221   Mexican five centavo 1905 – 1969
222   Mexican ten centavo
223   Mexican twenty centavo
224   Mexican one peso
225   Mexican fifty centavo
226   Mexican two, five, and ten pesos
227   Mexican one centavo 1899 –
        Two, five, ten pesos
230   Guatemala type coins starting 1915
235   Nicaragua type coins starting 1870
240   Cuba type coins starting 1915

DANSCO FOLDERS –

330   Australian halfpenny
331   Australian penny
332   Australian threepence and sixpence
333   Australian shilling
334   Australian florin
337   Australia type coins
350   Fiji complete collection
360   New Guinea complete collection
371   Irish farthings, halfpennies, and pennies
372   Irish threepence, sixpence, and shillings
373   Irish florins and half crowns

440   New Zealand halfpenny and penny
442   New Zealand threepence and sixpence
443   New Zealand shilling and florin
444   New Zealand half crown and crown
447   New Zealand Type
450   Hong Kong type collection
452   Panama type collection
460   Japan type collection 1870-

500   Swiss Confederation type set

600   Israel type set 1948-

Whitman

Whitman Publishing had a fantastic line of coin folders and albums; up to the 1970s they produced (by my estimation) no fewer than 141 types of folders and 86 types of albums! The stock number system used by Whitman followed certain logic and one can see how the series developed over time by looking at the stock numbers. Unfortunately, in recent years the company has reused some of the stock numbers that had been utilized on discontinued albums. The list below details the folders and albums that were produced up to the 1970s.

There are some intriguing gaps in some of the stock numbers, particularly in the British folders that carry a stock number in the 8000 range. It leads me to wonder if more folders were planned, but shelved due to declining popularity of the folders. The Whitman stock numbers can be broken down as follows:

8000s: Coin folders for British, Irish, Channel Islands
9000s: Coin folders for United States, Canada
9100s: One-a-year series
9400s: Coin albums for United States, World
9500s: Coin albums for various countries
9600s: Coin folders for Australian, British, British Commonwealth, and Mexico (major exception: folder 9699, Kennedy half 1964-)

Whitman folders:

8001	British farthings, blank
8002	British halfpennies, blank
8003	British pennies, blank
8004	British threepence brass, blank
8005	British sixpence, blank
8006	British shillings, blank
8008	British half crowns, blank
8009	British florins, 1911-1940
8010	British florins, 1941-1967
8011	British florins, blank
8012	British half crowns, 1911-1940
8013	British half crowns, 1941-1967

WHITMAN FOLDERS –

8020	Irish farthings 1928-1959
8021	Irish halfpennies 1929-1967
8022	Irish pennies 1928-1968
8023	Irish threepence 1928-1968
8024	Irish sixpence 1928-1968
8025	Irish shillings 1928-1968
8026	Irish florins 1928-1968
8027	Irish half crowns 1928-1967
8028	Jersey $1/26^{th}$ & $1/24^{th}$ shilling 1866-1947
8029	Jersey $1/13^{th}$ & $1/12^{th}$ shilling 1877-1966
8030	Guernsey One & two doubles 1830-1929
8031	Guernsey four doubles 1864-1956
8032	Guernsey Eight doubles, threepence 1864-1959
9000	Lincoln Memorial 1959-
9001	Large cent 1793-1825
9002	Large cent 1826-1857
9003	Indian Eagle cents 1857-1909
9004	Lincoln cents 1909-1940
9005	Half dime 1794-1873
9006	Shield type nickel 1866-1883
9007	Liberty head nickel 1883-1912
9008	Buffalo nickel 1913-1938
9009	Jefferson nickel 1938-1961
9010	Bust type dime 1796-1837
9011	Liberty seated dime 1837-1862
9012	Liberty seated dime 1863-1891
9013	Barber dime 1892-1916
9014	Mercury head dime 1916-1945
9015	Barber quarter 1892-1905
9016	Barber quarter 1906-1916
9017	Liberty Standing quarter 1916-1930
9018	Washington head quarter 1932-1945
9019	Barber half 1892-1903
9020	Barber half 1904-1916
9021	Liberty standing half 1916-1936

WHITMAN FOLDERS –

9022　Half cent 1793-1857
9023　Three cent silver 1851-1873
9024　Two cent & nickel three cent 1864-1889
9025　Dollars blank
9026A Type coins, small denominations
9026B Type coins, large denominations
9027　Liberty standing half 1937-1947
9028　Peace dollars 1921-1935
9029　Roosevelt dime 1946-
9030　Lincoln cent 1941-
9031　Washington head quarter 1946-1959
9032　Franklin half 1948-1963
9033　Liberty seated quarter 1838-1865
9034　Liberty seated quarter 1866-1891
9035　Liberty seated half 1839-1850
9036　Liberty seated half 1851-1862
9037　Liberty seated half 1862-1873
9038　Liberty seated half 1873-1891
9040　Washington head quarter 1960-
9041　Cents, blank
9042　Nickels, blank
9043　Dimes, blank
9044　Quarters, blank
9045　Halves, blank
9046　Twentieth century type coins
9061　Canadian large cents 1858-1920
9062　Canadian small cents 1920-
9063　Canadian silver five cents 1858-1921
9064　Canadian nickel five cents 1922-1960
9065　Canadian ten cents 1858-1936
9066　Canadian ten cents 1937-
9067　Canadian twenty-five cents 1858-1910
9068　Canadian twenty-five cents 1911-1952
9069　Canadian twenty-five cents 1953-
9070　Canadian fifty cents 1870-1910

WHITMAN FOLDERS –

9071   Canadian fifty cents 1911-1936
9072   Canadian fifty cents 1937-1960
9073   Canadian dollars 1935-1957
9074   Cents and half cents of British North America
9075   Newfoundland five cents 1865-1947
9076   Newfoundland ten cents 1865-1947
9077   Newfoundland twenty and twenty-five cents 1865-1919
9078   Newfoundland fifty cents, 1870-1919
9079   Canadian twenty-five cents blank
9080   Canadian fifty cents blank
9081   Canada type coin collection
9082   Morgan dollar 1878-1883
9083   Morgan dollar 1884-1890
9084   Morgan dollar 1891-1897
9085   Morgan dollar 1898-1921
9086   Canadian dollars blank
9087   Canadian dollars 1958-
9088   Newfoundland type coin collection
9089   Canadian nickel five cents 1961-
9094   Canadian fifty cents 1961-
9100   Cents, one-a-year, 1909-
9102   Nickels, one-a-year, 1913-
9103   Dimes, one-a-year, 1916-
9104   Quarters, one-a-year, 1916-

Whitman albums:
9400   Half cents 1793-1857
9401   Large cents 1793-1857
9402   Indian cents 1856-1909
9405   Lincoln cents 1909-1940
9406   Lincoln cents 1941-
9407   Liberty nickels 1883-1912
9408   Buffalo nickels 1913-1938
9410   Jefferson nickels 1938-1964
9411   Liberty seated half dimes 1837-1873

WHITMAN ALBUMS –

9412   Liberty dimes 1892-1916
9413   Mercury dime 1916-1945
9414   Roosevelt dime 1946-
9415   Bust half 1807-1839
9416   Liberty quarters 1892-1916
9417   Liberty standing quarters 1916-1930
9418   Washington quarters 1932-1964
9420   Liberty half 1892-1906
9421   Liberty half 1907-1915
9422   Kennedy half 1964-
9423   Liberty walking half 1916-1940
9424   Liberty walking half 1941-1947
9425   Franklin half 1948-1963
9426   Trade dollars 1873-1883
9427   Morgan dollars 1878-1886
9428   Morgan dollars 1887-1896
9429   Morgan dollars 1897-1921
9430   Peace dollars 1921-1935
9432   Year sets, blank
9433   Commemoratives
9434   Type set, half cents to quarters
9435   Type set, halves and dollars
9436   Type set, gold coins
9436   Two cents, three cents, shield five cents and twenty cents
9437   Liberty seated dimes 1837-1891
9439   Liberty seated quarters 1838-1865
9440   Liberty seated quarters 1866-1891
9441   Cents, blank – 120 ports
9442   Nickels, blank – 96 ports
9443   Dimes, plain – 120 ports
9444   Quarters, blank – 84 ports
9445   Half dollars, blank – 64 ports
9446   Dollars, blank – 36 ports
9447   Liberty seated half 1839-1863
9448   Liberty seated half 1864-1891

WHITMAN ALBUMS –

9449   Modern mint sets – mint sealed
9450   Modern proof sets – mint sealed
9452   Civil War tokens 1861-1865
9454   Crowns of the world
9455   Miscellaneous tokens
9456   Miscellaneous medals
9459   Around-the-world, volume I
9460   Around-the-world, volume II
9500   Canadian large cents 1858-1920
9501   Canadian small cents 1920-
9502   Canadian five cent silver 1858-1921
9503   Canadian five cent nickel 1922-
9504   Canadian ten cents 1858-
9505   Canadian twenty and twenty-five cents 1870-1936
9506   Canadian twenty-five cents 1937-
9507   Canadian twenty-five cents blank
9508   Canadian fifty cents 1870-1936
9509   Canadian fifty cents 1937-
9510   Canadian fifty cents blank
9511   Canadian dollars 1935-1965
9512   Canadian dollars blank
9513   Canadian type set
9514   Newfoundland type set
9515   Canadian mint-sealed mint sets
9516   British type minor coins, 1902-
9517   British type silver coins, 1902-
9518   Panama type set 1904-1960s
9520   British type Queen Victoria, 1837-1901
9521   Canadian type set large denominations
9522   Canadian type set small denominations
9524   Mexican type set 1905-
9526   Philippine type set 1864-1961
9527   Australian type, bronze and decimal coins
9528   Australian type, silver coins
9530   British farthings, 1860-1901

WHITMAN ALBUMS and FOLDERS –

9531   British farthings, 1902-1956
9532   British halfpennies, 1860-1901
9533   British halfpennies, 1902-1936
9534   British halfpennies, 1937-
9535   British pennies, 1860-1901
9536   British pennies, 1902-1936
9537   British pennies, 1937-

Whitman folders:
9661   Australian halfpennies 1911-1936
9662   Australian halfpennies 1938-1964
9663   Australian pennies 1911-1936
9664   Australian pennies 1938-1952
9665   Australian pennies 1953-1964
9666   Australian threepence 1910-1964
9667   Australian sixpence 1910-1963
9668   Australian shillings 1910-1936
9669   Australian shillings 1938-1963
9670   Australian florins 1910-1936
9671   Australian florins and crowns 1937-1963
9672   British Commonwealth farthing size coins
9673   British Commonwealth halfpenny size coins
9674   British Commonwealth penny size coins
9675   British farthings, 1860-1901
9676   British farthings, 1902-1936
9677   British farthings, 1937-1956
9678   British halfpennies, 1860-1901
9679   British halfpennies, 1902-1936
9680   British halfpennies, 1937-1967
9681   British pennies, 1860-1880
9682   British pennies, 1881-1901
9683   British pennies, 1902-1929
9684   British pennies, 1930-1967
9685   British threepence silver, 1838-1901
9686   British threepence silver, 1902-1945

WHITMAN FOLDERS –

9687   British threepence brass, 1937-1967
9689   British sixpence, 1902-1936
9690   British sixpence, 1937-1967
9693   British shillings, 1902-1936
9694   British shillings, 1937-1951
9695   British shillings, 1953-1967
9696   Mexican one centavo 1905 -
9697   Mexican five centavos 1905-1955
9698   Mexican five centavos 1954-
9699   Kennedy half 1964-

9800   Coin size testing chart

Bibliography

Bresset, Ken. *A Guide Book of English Coins: Nineteenth and Twentieth Centuries.* 9th ed. Racine, WI: Whitman Publishing Co., 1982.

Charlton, J. E. *Standard Catalogue of Canadian Coins and Paper Money.* 15th ed. Racine, WI: Whitman Publishing Co., 1966.

De Clermont, Andre P. and John Wheeler. *Spink's Catalogue of British Colonial and Commonwealth Coins.* London: Spink and Son Ltd., 1986.

Divo, Jean-Paul and Edwin Tobler. *Die Münzen der Schweiz im 19. und 20. Jahrhundert.* Zürich: Bank Leu & Co. AG, 1967.

Krause, Chester L. and Clifford Mishler. *Standard Catalog of World Coins: Deluxe ANA Centennial Edition.* Iola, WI: Krause Publications, 1991.

Norges Mynter perioden 1814-2000. 31st ed. Skien, Norway: Nordfrim Norge, 2000.

Sieg, Frovin. *Siegs Møntkatalog Norden.* 14th ed. Roslev, Denmark: Salling Bogtrykkeri, 1983

Tonkin, Archie. *Myntboken 1991.* Nr. 21. Linköping, Sweden: Tonkin AB, 1991.

Vice, David. *The Coinage of British West Africa & St. Helena 1684-1958.* Birmingham, England: Format Publications, 1983.

www.ingramcontent.com/pod-product-compliance
Lightning Source LLC
LaVergne TN
LVHW091157080426
835509LV00006B/724